ARNHEM
LIFT
A GERMAN JEW
IN THE GLIDER PILOT REGIMENT

To all who fell at Arnhem – Allied and German

'I crawled right under the brushwood and saw and heard the bullets splashing the ground and hitting the branches and tree stumps all round me. I was sure this was going to be the end and kicked myself for doing such an idiotic thing; trying to take a strong German position on my own. I swore that if ever I got out of this hopeless position I would never again be such a bloody fool. I lay completely still, bullets whizzing about me. I wondered if I wanted to pray; that is what everybody is supposed to do in a position like this; but I just did not feel like it, and to calm and steady myself I watched a colony of ants go about their well-planned and systematic business.'

ARNHEM LIFT

A GERMAN JEW
IN THE GLIDER PILOT REGIMENT

LOUIS HAGEN

SPELLMOUNT

The action recorded here took place between 17 September and 25 September 1944. *Arnhem Lift* was first published in January 1945 (without the author's knowledge!). Not only is it an extraordinary story, dealing as it does with a German Jewish refugee who ends up flying a Horsa into the disaster, it is also believed to be the very first book published about the battle – to the fury of the military and to great public acclaim. In 1950, Louis Hagen married Anne Mie, a Norwegian artist, with whom he had two daughters, Siri and Caroline. Dividing his time between London and Norway, Louis Hagen established Primrose Film Productions and went on to create 25 children's films. He returned to Arnhem twice, first in 1948 to show his fiancée where he had fought, and again in 1994 for the 50th Anniversary. He had not planned to attend as he felt 'the idea of parading with hundreds of old veterans like myself wearing rows of medals and red berets did not appeal.' Louis Hagen died on 17 August 2000 at the age of 84. He rests at Asker in Oslo, Norway.

First published 1945. This edition published 2012
by Spellmount, an imprint of

The History Press
The Mill, Brimscombe Port
Stroud, Gloucestershire, GL5 2QG
www.thehistorypress.co.uk

British Library Cataloguing in Publication Data.
A catalogue record for this book is available from the British Library.

ISBN 978 0 7524 6868 6

Typesetting and origination by The History Press
Manufacturing Managed by Jellyfish Print Solutions Ltd.
Printed in Malta.

CONTENTS

ACKNOWLEDGEMENTS

With thanks to Jean Medawar, my oldest friend, who first taught me to speak English, and now helped me to write it.

I want to thank my old friend Vivian Milroy for his patient help and detailed research into the strategies of the Battle of Arnhem.

I am grateful to my former 'enemy', Major Winrich Behr, for telling me his experiences at Arnhem and for letting me use them in this book.

Louis Hagen, 1993

PREFATORY NOTE TO
THE FIRST EDITION

When the author of this book arrived home on leave, after fighting right through the Arnhem action, everybody wanted to hear his story. After telling it several times, he began to find the repetition irksome, so he spent the rest of his leave writing it all down, while the events were still vivid in his mind. Any more friends who asked him for the story would get a type-written document! That is his explanation of how it came to be written.

Then someone suggested he should publish it. A copy arrived on my desk. After glancing through a few pages, I settled down to an absorbed reading of what I found to be a remarkable piece of reporting. Other urgent matters were left aside, and willy nilly I had to read on to the end. I believe that other readers will find it equally compelling.

This young soldier had no public in mind, beyond a few personal friends, when he set down his adventures. This may account for the intimate quality of his writing. But there can be no doubt he has a flair for picking out those details and moments which we all want to hear about – the touches of unexpected realism which help us to visualise and live over again the incredible heroic episode of Arnhem.

I have struck nothing quite like this diary for giving the actual feel and flavour of modern war at its most spectacular. This is the story of one man's battle. It doesn't purport to describe the action as a whole. It gives instead a series of ultra-vivid images and experiences. Like real life, it is inconsequent and surprising. It is also straightforward and free from egoism. In spite of the grim nature of the ordeal, the author seems to have come through with a sense of elation rather than with the despair and nervous exhaustion which the First World War seems to have produced in most of those who have written about it. This resilience gives an effect of balance and composure to the story, which is very remarkable considering the hectic and often horrible things that happen throughout it.

C.M., 1945

FOREWORD TO THE
SECOND EDITION

This is the story of the First British Airborne Division's great fight to hold the Arnhem Bridge as seen and experienced by a Glider Pilot.

It is my purpose here to paint very briefly the bigger picture of the Airborne Operations in Holland, a picture which only the gallant survivors were to learn from me when they returned to Nijmegen after their withdrawal from the Arnhem perimeter.

The Second Army was faced with increasing opposition by re-formed German Battle Groups, in difficult country and with a series of water obstacles barring the way into Germany. Winter was approaching. The First British Airborne Corps (First British Airborne Division, 82nd US Airborne Division and 101st US Airborne Division) were ordered to seize and capture a corridor over 40 miles long which included the great bridges at Grave (River Maas), Nijmegen (River Waal) and Arnhem (Neder Rijn). The Second Army was to drive through this corridor and debouch into the North German plains, thereby turning the defences of the Rhine.

The Airborne Operation was successful in capturing the corridor and bridges, except for the essential gap between Nijmegen and Arnhem bridges. Owing primarily to the almost uncanny recovery by the German Army which had just suffered defeat in Normandy and on the Seine, and bad weather for air operations after the first two days, the Second Army were unable to reach Arnhem Bridge in time to achieve the complete breakthrough and the relief of the hard-pressed First Airborne Division.

This Division's outstanding action and the successful operations of the two fine American Airborne Divisions, though failing in their final object of passing the Second Army through into Germany, ensured the retention and consolidation of the high ground at Nijmegen, pushed the Second Army, with incredibly few casualties, through over the 40 miles of difficult country and over two great rivers, and provided the springboard from which 21 Army Group launched its final assault on Germany early the next year.

Without the First Airborne Division's heroic stand at Arnhem, which protected the northern flank of the battle and contained considerable German reserves, no such results would have been possible.

Lieutenant-General Sir Frederick A.M. Browning KBE, CB, DSO
October 1952

1

ABOUT THE AUTHOR

When I fought in the Battle of Arnhem, I was a lighthearted young German who had been born into a wealthy Jewish family of bankers. I had been brought up by liberal and devoted parents in idyllic surroundings near Potsdam, on the outskirts of Berlin, a lovely small town where the Prussian royal families had for centuries spent their summers in elegant and luxurious houses on the shores of Lake Jungfernsee.

Now I am an Englishman nearing 80, [Louis is writing this in 1993] still lighthearted, married, with two children and two grandchildren, living comfortably in Highgate, six miles from the centre of London.

This book tells the story of the events that were partly responsible for my transformation.

When I was a boy I was so full of the physical joys of life that I learned very little at school. I was more interested in 'taking dares'. I was dared to come into class with a false beard, or riding on a horse. I was dared to eat a live frog. I did all these things, and my reports were very bad. My parents decided it was a waste of time to keep me at school. One day, when I was about sixteen years old, I heard my father say to my mother, 'There's no point in torturing the boy any longer. We'd better enrol him as an apprentice engineer.' So I left school and went to start at the bottom in the BMW works, where my father and grandfather were on the board of directors. I enjoyed this new working environment and I learned a lot, without losing my high spirits.

One day I stupidly wrote a vulgar postcard about Hitler's Brownshirts to my sister Nina.* She left it lying around and it was picked up by one of the maids. This maid had been stealing my mother's jewellery and was about to be sacked. She threatened to take the card to her boyfriend – who was one of Hitler's storm troopers – unless my mother withdrew the accusation of stealing.

This was in 1934 and neither of my parents had any idea how seriously the new National Socialist authorities would treat the incident. So the maid was sacked; she went to her boyfriend, and soon after that storm troopers appeared at the BMW factory to arrest me. I was taken under guard and shut up in Torgau, an old castle which had been turned into a concentration camp. I was with a mixed group of men who were considered 'racially inferior' like Jews or Gypsies, or were thought to be politically dangerous, like communists and freemasons. The camp was run by Nazi storm troopers who enjoyed humiliating and torturing elderly Jews, or boys like me who had been brought up with more money and education then they had enjoyed. I was kicked off my straw palliasse in the middle of the night and made to crawl about naked on all fours while I was beaten for the amusement of the drunken guards. We had to empty latrines with our bare hands and carry the contents away in heavy iron containers that cut into the skin of our palms.

---

* The note read 'Toilet paper is now forbidden, so there are even more Brown Shirts.'

I was comforted by a fat, middle-aged communist called Wolfgang who became my friend. One day, while I was playing chess with Wolfgang, I noticed a group of men crowding round the window facing the courtyard. We got up to see what they were looking at but before I could get there Wolfgang pulled me back: 'There's nothing there, Budi. Let's get on with the game.' But I insisted on seeing what was happening: if ever I got out, I wanted to be able to tell people what was going on.

What was happening was the cruellest, most shocking thing I have ever seen. It was a very hot, sunny day; a group of SA men in shirt-sleeves were standing round the farmyard pond where there were usually a few ducks swimming and a couple of pigs cooling themselves in the mud. There were neither ducks nor pigs in the pond, but instead four prisoners splashing around, entirely covered in mud, moving as if in slow motion because of its dragging weight. They were trying to crawl out of the pond but whenever they reached the edge, the SA men kicked them back in, laughing and shouting. I could not go on watching and turned away. Later I learnt that none of them survived.

When the guards could think of nothing better to do, they gave each of us a bucket of water, then chased us round the courtyard. If we spilt any, they beat us. I was young and very fit and I managed, but some of the older men were soon exhausted in the blistering heat and collapsed. They were then kicked and beaten until they got up and started running again. The weakest were chased into the muddy pond to 'cool down' before, covered in mud, they had to start running again.*

After six weeks of this I was rescued. One day, standing to attention in the courtyard, I saw the gates open. A large black Mercedes drove through, flying the swastika flag. In it was the father of one of my

---

* The description of murder in the duck pond is taken from Louis Hagen's unpublished biography.

friends at school – a judge.* I heard him ask for me. I was escorted to the guard-house where the Commandant informed me that if I ever revealed what was going on in the castle 'We will get you, wherever you are, and bring you back, and then you will never get out.'

After my concentration camp experience my parents realised how dangerous it was for their five children to stay in Germany; my father thought it unnecessary, however, to make preparations for himself and my mother to leave. He used to say 'This Hitler business is too crazy; it won't last'. He thought the Nazis would not do anything to him because he had been decorated when a naval officer in the First World War and was head of one of the oldest and most respected banking families.

Arrangements were made to get me out of Germany as quickly as possible. It was not easy, in spite of my family's many connections abroad, because at this time thousands of Jews were also desperately trying to leave. One country after another tried to control the flood of refugees from Germany; they all had problems with unemployment and were in a severe economic depression. It was almost eighteen months before a business friend of my father, Sir Andrew McFadyean, arranged for me to emigrate to England in January, 1936.

Sir Andrew, Chairman of the Liberal Party, was adept at getting German refugees into England: among others, he rescued the Hamburg banker, Sigmund Warburg, who founded the well-known London bank, S.G. Warburg. Sir Andrew managed to get me a job with the Pressed Steel Company at Cowley, near Oxford, which made car bodies for Austin, Morris and other British car manufacturers. I found that my apprenticeship at BMW helped me a great deal.

The job lasted almost three years. Then one day I was summoned to see Mr Muller, the Managing Director. He told me with some

---

* This was the father of Claus Furhmann, a boy Louis had befriended at school. Apparently the relationship then was mutually beneficial, Claus helping Louis with his school work, Louis acting as Claus's minder. Though Louis could not have known at that time quite how beneficial the friendship would prove to be.

embarrassment that no foreigners were now allowed to work in factories engaged in war work; he had no option but to dismiss me. He assured me that he deeply regretted this because he had only had good reports about my work. He asked me what my private circumstances were and what I would do now. I told him that I had no family in England and no private money because my family were not allowed to send money out of Germany, and that my permit was valid only for the Pressed Steel Company. Mr Muller arranged for my salary of £3 per week to continue and promised that he would try to help me.

Ironically, only three years earlier the Managing Director of BMW, Herr Popper, had called me to his office and told me that one of the most embarrassing things he had ever had to do was to dismiss me – the Ministry of War would not in future permit 'non-Aryans' to work in factories producing armaments.

Mr Muller soon arranged for me to be transferred to the sales and service department of a subsidiary, Prestcold Refrigerators, in London. But when war broke out even this job folded because I was then officially classified as an 'Enemy Alien'.

Now I was jobless I kept myself busy as a carpenter, building stage sets for small experimental and club theatres. I got hardly any pay and had to give up my flat, so I stayed with various friends and often slept on the stage wrapped in one of the curtains. I actually enjoyed this free and easy life.

I was of course elated at the prospect of the Nazis' downfall and like most of my friends, I went to one of the many recruiting offices to volunteer for the army. An officer there told me that I would be informed when and where I was to join His Majesty's Forces. As all the others who had volunteered were awaiting their call-up papers, I was not worried when I did not hear anything for a long time.

At last I did get a notice, forwarded by Sir Andrew, to appear at a tribunal to decide whether I was an anti-Nazi or a dangerous enemy alien, to be interned for the duration of the war. Sir Andrew offered to appear at this tribunal, but I told him I did not think this was necessary as my case was so clear – I was of Jewish extraction and had been imprisoned in a Nazi concentration camp.

When I appeared at the tribunal, the chairman, before he even asked me to sit down, barked at me, 'How is it you arrived here in your own car?* You were supposed to report regularly to the police, not to be away from your home overnight and not to travel more than five miles from your registered address. You complied with none of these regulations and the police were only able to trace you through Sir Andrew McFadyean.' He went on dressing me down for several minutes. Luckily for me Sir Andrew had decided to attend the tribunal and now offered to testify on my behalf. He said that he had known me and my family for over fifteen years, that I had no close family in this country and had only English friends, and therefore had not realised that aliens had been supposed to register with the police when the war started. His testimony saved me from internment – probably in Australia or Canada – and after a further strong reprimand from the chairman I was free, until my call-up, to return to my jolly life in the theatre.

It did not last long, however. A few days later I was arrested as a deserter because I had not reported for military service. I was stuck in a cell in Notting Hill police station. Without a fixed address, I had of course never received the call-up notice. My guardian angel, Sir Andrew, again saved me and, after I had spent two nights in the cells, I was escorted by military police to the Pioneer Corps training camp at Westward Ho! near Bideford in Devon. The other recruits cheered when I answered my name at the next morning's roll-call. For weeks they had got used to the dead silence whenever my name had been called.

I soon caught up with the military training, marching, polishing boots and brasses, laying out equipment, making my bed accurate to the millimetre and presenting arms with broomsticks. We were

---

★ Enemy aliens were forbidden to own or drive cars.

not issued with rifles because there were not enough for the huge number of recruits – and possibly because we were not yet entirely trusted. Nor could we yet hope to become commissioned or non-commissioned officers. By the time the British Expeditionary Force was being evacuated across the Channel from Dunkirk, we so-called Pioneers were stationed along the Devon coast defending our newly adopted country with sticks and clubs. But it was a lovely hot summer and we swam and sunned ourselves whether we were on guard duty or not.

When our initial training was over we were sent to dig latrines in remote open country where airfields and army depots were to be built. Although the work was hard and we were often very wet and cold, we were in good spirits. At last, and at least, we were doing something to defeat German fascism. Most of us came from an educated Jewish middle class, so there was none of the usual barrack-room obscenity. Everyone was most civilised and one often heard conversations like this:'Nehmen Sie bitten den Eimer, Herr Doktor. Er ist aber sehr schwer';'Vielen Dank, Herr Professor. Ich schaffe es schon.' (Please take the bucket, Doctor, but it is very heavy';'Many thanks, Professor, I think I can manage.')

We were a strange collection – professions, academics and a few musicians and writers – and our motto was light-hearted:'Vy vorry? Ve vill vin ze var'.

Slowly the War Office began to trust us (as far as I know there was not a single case of espionage among the 15,000 or so 'enemy aliens' in the British forces during the entire war), and one by one other units and regiments became open to us. I soon found out that I was not the type for a military career and decided to volunteer for anything that would relieve the boredom and might teach me something or offer me a new experience.

First I volunteered for the Army Fire Brigade, then for the Ordnance Corps, then the REME (Corps of Royal Electrical and Mechanical Engineers), the Artillery Assault Corps, and many others.

I was invariably accepted; I was the right age and physique and I could read and write. The many journeys to and from these selection boards gave me plenty of opportunity to get lost on the way so that I could visit my friends in London and Oxford.

One of the very last regiments that was prepared to accept 'enemy aliens' was the Army Air Corps' Glider Pilot Regiment, which was officially formed on 24 February 1942. Of course I immediately volunteered for this: to become a pilot was the ultimate goal, not only for me, but also for thousands of other soldiers of all ranks.

I have never been to an interview in such a state of excitement. I felt that if I was accepted I would be the luckiest man alive. I still remember how I disliked being treated as a third-class citizen in Germany and a foreigner in Britain. Becoming a British pilot would be a miraculous change.

When I stood in front of the selection board I was trembling, and when the chairman, a colonel asked me, 'Where do you come from?' I became speechless. If I said 'Potsdam' would I have to go into a lengthy and complicated explanation? If I said 'Oxford' would they call me a liar?

'Relax, man, and answer. We're not going to bite you,' the colonel said, smiling. His easy manner brought me back to my senses. So I said 'Potsdam, Sir' and after a moment of surprise he asked me to explain. I did so and then he said, 'My second question would have been, "Why did you volunteer?" but that of course is obvious.'

Two weeks later (it was now late in 1943) I was queuing up for my flying gear at the RAF airfield at Denham, just outside London. Flying did not come easily to me and it was rumoured that unless we were ready to go solo after seven hours' tuition in the air we were 'out' and would have to return to our army units. Luckily I had a kind and understanding instructor.

We trained in the famous de Havilland Tiger Moth, a beautiful open two-seater biplane designed in 1923. Day after day flying lessons went on, some lasting for only a quarter of an hour. Every minute in the air was recorded in my log-book, but as the seven hours crept nearer, I could not imagine being all by myself. When the flight book recorded eight hours and fifteen minutes my instructor jumped out of his seat and said, 'It's all yours. I don't dare to watch. I'm going to have a cup of tea in the canteen.'

I took off and stopped thinking of anything else except flying. It was suddenly a wonderful feeling to be all by myself in the endless sky. I flew the prescribed circuit inspired by the joy of flying alone. My landing was OK – not perfect, but good enough not to damage the undercarriage. I was over the first hurdle.

But we could not get our 'wings' until we had passed tests on the theory of navigation, aircraft recognition and the principles of flight. I did not find this easy and had to spend all my spare time revising. I was continually interrupted by kit and rifle inspections, interminable drill parades and random roll-calls organised by a sadistic Army sergeant-major who was determined that we should not succumb to the lax RAF ways.

One day I was studying hard in my Nissen hut when the door was flung open and the sergeant-major barked out, 'You lazy lout! Why aren't you on parade?' I explained that I had been excused parades so that I could get ready for the next test. 'You've got all night to do that,' he said 'I wish I had,' I replied, 'but your stupid regulations mean we have to be in bed with lights out at ten o'clock.' He stared at me, then roared, 'Now you're insulting a superior officer. You'll regret this, young man. Report to Company Office, 1830 hours.' I realised that the sergeant-major had had it in for me for some time. And the Duty Officer sided with him – without even asking for my side of the story. 'We don't need people like you,' he said coldly. 'Hand in your kit. Get your travelling papers and return to your unit. Dismiss!'

I went to say goodbye to my instructor. All he said was, 'What nonsense! We can't lose good chaps like you. I'll talk to the Squadron Leader.' I spent a very long and tense ten minutes. Then he came back, patted me on the shoulder and said, 'Go back to the stores and collect your gear before it's issued to someone else.' I could have hugged him, but made do with a half-choked 'Thank you, Sir.'

Before I got my wings as a second pilot, a new directive announced that all Germans and Austrians in front-line units had to be issued with new identity papers, with English-sounding names and British places of birth and next-of-kin. The reason for this was that, if any of us were taken prisoner and the Germans discovered our nationality, we would be tortured for information and then shot as traitors.

I went home to Oxford and there my closest friends, Jean and Peter Medawar,* suggested the name 'Lewis Haig' – a name I kept until a year or two after the war. The army thought it a great name because of the even more famous whisky. I was registered as born in Oxford and the Medawars were listed as my next-of-kin.

I never got my First-Class Glider Pilot wings because, on 17 September, 1944, we were ordered into action. Our destination was Arnhem, a small Dutch town on the lower Rhine. What happened then is described from Chapter three onwards.

---

*   Later Sir Peter Medawar, OM, CH, CBE (1915–1987), the distinguished medical scientist and Nobel Laureate.

2

THE BACKGROUND

After five long years of a land war against Germany, which had flowed from Poland to the Low Countries, Scandinavia and France, North Africa, Greece and Italy, the focus moved back to Britain in 1944. Here, in June of that year, the joint American/British forces mounted the greatest sea/air invasion in history. Three million men, half a million motor vehicles and tanks and three complete mobile harbours were ferried or flown or towed over 100 miles of English Channel.

It was not easy. In three days the Allies lost over 3000 troops – but a bridgehead 2 miles wide and 3 miles deep was established in Normandy. General Dwight Eisenhower, the Allied Supreme Commander, now commanded two and a quarter million men, who, in the next few weeks, were to advance through France against the tough and battle-hardened German troops.

As they advanced, the problems of supply grew. Half a million motor vehicles and armour needed a vast amount of petrol, oil and ammunition; and two and a quarter million men needed a constant supply of food, ammunition and equipment. Everything had to be shipped over the Channel either to the temporary Mulberry harbours, or on to bare beaches and then on to lorries for delivery to the forward units, the Allied bombing having put the French railways out of action. The supply lines soon stretched to the point where the advancing Allied troops had to slow down: they finally came to a halt at the beginning of September near the Dutch/Belgian border.

Now there was a new danger. A large army just standing still might well encourage the enemy to counter-attack: then, with winter coming on, the battle could develop into the bloody and inconclusive stalemate of trench warfare.

In order to break the deadlock, Field-Marshal Sir Bernard Montgomery, commanding 21st Army Group, the northern 'prong' of the Allied advance, proposed early in September 1944, using airborne troops to make a daring leap over the German defences and open up the way for a mass advance by the Allied armour into Germany. British and American parachutists and glider-borne troops would land in strength behind the German lines in Holland, capture bridges over the Meuse, Waal and Lower Rhine, and hold them while Lieutenant-General Miles Dempsey's British Second Army, led by XXX Corps, poured through Holland into Germany. Montgomery persuaded Eisenhower to support his plan, which went ahead under the codename 'Market Garden'.

The details of the plan, as evolved by Montgomery with Eisenhower's approval, called for the following:

Parachutists of US 101st Airborne Division would capture the canal bridges at Son and Veghel.

US 82nd Airborne Division would take the bridges over the River Maas at Grave and the River Waal at Nijmegen.

The bridge over the Lower Rhine at Arnhem – the farthest bridge – would be the responsibility of British 1st Airborne Division.

Simultaneously with the air landings, Lieutenant-General Brian Horrocks' XXX Corps would strike out northwards from the Neerpelt bridgehead and relieve the airborne troops in turn once they had captured the various bridges.

If successful the operation would establish an extended supply line as far as the last bridge at Arnhem. The great natural barrier, the Rhine, would have been crossed, and the Ruhr and the rest of Germany would lie open to the Second Army with no more natural obstacles in the way.

The details of that part of the plan which concerned Arnhem were worked out by Lieutenant-General Frederick ('Boy') Browning and Major-General Roy Urquhart, respectively the commanders of the British 1 Airborne Corps and 1st Airborne Division. (The two American airborne divisions were to come under Browning's 1 Airborne Corps for 'Market Garden'.) One factor that gave them some concern was that the RAF had insisted on the drops being made well outside the town, in order to avoid the anti-aircraft guns that were protecting Deelen airfield. Urquhart was unhappy about this, but such was the urgency that it was by then too late to refer the plan back to Montgomery.

The 1st Airborne Division plan called for 1 Parachute Brigade to capture and hold, in order, the Arnhem railway bridge, west of the town, a pontoon bridge about 2½ miles east of that, and, finally, the crucial road bridge 600 yards further to the east. 1 Airlanding Brigade would protect the landing-zones until the second wave, which would include 4 Parachute Brigade, landed on the second day; they would then move east to link up with 1 Parachute Brigade, who would be holding the bridges. 1 Airlanding Brigade would then move to the west and form a defensive wall. Finally, Polish 1 Independent Parachute Brigade would land south of the river on the third day and march over the bridge to join up with 1 Parachute Brigade.

The bulk of the division – some 10,000 men in all – with their weapons and equipment, were to be landed in three stages on 17, 18 and 19 September on two landing-zones and two drop-zones situated from 6 to 10 miles to the north-east of Arnhem, in the neighbourhood of the hamlets of Wolfheze and Heelsum.

A number of supply and reinforcement drops were also planned, to be activated as the situation demanded. If all went well the Division would be relieved by Horrocks' XXX Corps within two days. Even under the most unfavourable circumstances they would expect the operation to be over in four days. The path would then be clear for the bulk of Second Army to pour up the corridor, occupy Holland and turn east into the industrial Ruhr.

3

ARNHEM LIFT

Anyone who went to Arnhem could have told this kind of story. Mine is for the friends and relations of the men who did not come back ...

Monday

We knew it was coming off this time as the first glider lift had left on Saturday morning. We were waiting in the mess for the tug pilots to return and give us the gen. All seemed well. They had found the L.Z. – Landing Zone – quite easily, with no flak to complain about and, as far as they could see, there was no ground resistance. We were all happy and confident about our lift on Monday morning – this time we knew that it was not going to be cancelled, as once a large-scale airborne operation like this has started nothing can interfere with its planned development.

We were lucky to be one of the first planes to take off on Monday morning. I was second pilot – the first pilot, Mac, was a typical Glaswegian. Our load consisted of one jeep with a trailer, both loaded with petrol, and three chaps of the Parachute Brigade. They rather resented coming with us because to them a glider is an unknown quantity and an extremely dangerous way of travelling. They feel much safer jumping with the other lads.

It is hard physical labour flying a glider in the slipstream of another aircraft, but our tug pilot was very skilful in avoiding the hundreds of other planes making for Holland. He had to fly completely out of formation and at the wrong altitude to achieve that, but we encouraged him and praised him all the way.

Map reading did not seem much use to us, once we got over the sea and were approaching Holland, as the Germans had flooded all the large islands in the Rhine delta and great stretches of the country itself were under water. Dry land was slowly emerging and I thought it time to check up on our position.

'Hello Tug ... Matchbox here ... How many minutes before we reach the LZ? Over.'

'Hello Matchbox ... Tug here ... Another fifteen minutes and it's all yours ... Can you pinpoint your position? ... Over.'

'Thank you, Tug ... I should say we were just crossing the first of the three arms of the Rhine delta ... Please confirm this ... Over to you.'

'You are correct ... Now only two more river crossings and you should see your LZ.'

From now till we landed it was essential that I should not lose our position for a moment. I continually checked from my map to the ground and peered searchingly forward for the first signs of our objective. Some flak came up at us, but it was very light. Our ideal pilot still kept us away from the rabble and out of any slipstream. I made a mental note to buy him a pint when we got back.

Soon I recognised the Lower Rhine, and a moment later could see our LZ – two small squares of wooded land pieced together at one corner only. Our landing was to be just where the woods joined together. It looked exactly like the photographs they had shown us at the briefing. I never imagined they could possibly look so much alike.

This was the moment to cast off:

'Hello Tug … We are getting ready to cast off now … Thanks for the wizard ride.'

'Best of luck, Matchbox … See you soon.'

'OK Tug … Same to you.'

Mac pulls the lever which releases the cables from our wings and we are in free flight. The tug banks off to the right as Mac pulls up our nose to gain height and reduce our flying speed. As we settle to our normal gliding speed, all the noise dies away and it seems unbelievably peaceful and calm in our cockpit. We can't think of it as other than one of our many mass landing exercises. We are now slowly losing height, and as we cross the river we can clearly see the bridge at Arnhem which is our ultimate objective.

We are nearly there now. We turn to starboard with half flaps down and our gliding angle steepens suddenly. Another 15 degrees to starboard and we are just about over our landing area. Full flaps down and our nose is now pointing directly to the ground, the flaps keeping our speed constant and just above stalling speed. Someone cuts in from the right and we veer off a little, and then, just before we hit the ground, pull out level. We lift gently over a hedge and then touch down firmly. Brakes full on … a slow skid to port … a perfect landing.

We sat there for a moment, looking pleased with ourselves, when the crackle of distant machine-guns and the whistle of some nearer shots that were obviously meant for us, reminded us forcibly that this time we were not on an exercise. We leapt out and got into the tail unit, which we had to remove before the jeep and trailer could be got out.

Mac and I start on the heavy bolts inside the tail, eight of them, and they have to be synchronised. Meanwhile, two of the parachutists loosen the shackles on the jeep and trailer, and the third one begins to cut the control wires. Mac and I are sweating like pigs. We have to work together and reach the same stage of the operation at the same time. We have to be quick. They are still sniping at us and we are completely helpless and exposed. Safety wire cut … backwards and forwards with the release lever … one by one the bolts come out … not so hard really … pretty much like the drill on the station … I'm stuck now … the bastards are getting more and more difficult … I'm so terribly hot. I send one of the parachutists to stick the trestle under the body and he shouts that he has done so … we get to the last two bolts … must be completely together now … mine is quite loose … ready Mac? … right … go! … why the hell doesn't the tail fall off? … we've done everything just like the practice … we bang from the inside but it is stuck fast. I jump out to look and discover that the bloody fool of a parachutist has stuck the trestle under the tail itself. … I kick it away, and with a terrific crash the whole tail fuselage breaks off and falls over on the trestle … it's in the way still … we all get our shoulders under it and heave to the left … but the trestle is jammed in the fuselage now and embedded in the ground … it's a hell of a job … eventually we manage it, sweating, cursing and using all our strength.

The two runners slipped out and fitted beautifully, and the paratroop driver drove straight out of the glider. As we jumped on the jeep and drove off, we noticed just on the right a cross and grave of one of yesterday's glider pilots. We had been surprisingly lucky. Most of the first and second lifts had taken a lot of punishment before they even reached the ground. We had not really done so badly because now that we had a chance to look around, everywhere we saw groups of men cursing, sweating and heaving to get the tails off their gliders. Some were even using saws and axes, and when we looked at our watches we found that we had done the job in 20 minutes, which made us feel very pleased with ourselves. To get to our first rendez-vous we had to follow a narrow sandy lane through low brushwood, small fields and single rows of trees. Everywhere we saw gliders; in the fields, some even on the trees, there were an odd wing wedged between two big branches of an oak, a tail unit sticking right up in the air, and pieces of gliders distributed everywhere. We passed a large meadow with gliders parked in a more orderly fashion; obviously this was the real landing zone of Sunday's lift. We joined more and more jeeps and trailers, all filing to their various RVs. Ours was not so difficult as it was Wolfheze station, and from there to the lunatic asylum. It was a tiny station and its main features were the cross-roads running over the lines and parallel to the railway. Here was a terrific assembly of jeeps, trailers, light artillery and groups of parachutists. Red Cross jeeps with stretchers bearing casualties were passing through, nurses and men vainly trying to repair the water system in between this confusion. All the while we were sniped at; sometimes a mortar would go over and everyone seemed to disappear, but after a few seconds the confusion returned. Everyone was spreading out maps and asking everyone if they had seen or heard of their respective units.

In the crowd I suddenly spotted a glider pilot of a different squadron whom I had been hoping to meet for months. He had taken unfair advantage of me one day when I was about to go on leave. The urge to get away, once a leave pass is in your pocket, is so strong that any sacrifice is temporarily justified. This chap had dashed up to me when the car was packed up and ready to take us to the station, and asked me for the loan of a couple of quid, promising to return it by post, as we were unlikely to meet again. I never heard of him again and was very indignant, as he knew that I had no means of getting hold of him. I thought it was a dirty trick. There he was in the middle of the cross-roads at Wolfheze, and it all came back to me, and besides I had only ten shillings and no Dutch money on me. Sniping or no sniping, I started to dun him. He protested that he had very little cash on him, and an animated financial discussion proceeded. My troop shouted at me to come on as I had all the maps; they added that I could continue my argument when I got back to Whitechapel. We suddenly realised how idiotic we must look and both burst out laughing. He pressed a few guilders into my hand and I joined my troop again. We glider pilots were supposed to remain with the units we had taken over until further orders, and so we arrived eventually at the main building of the lunatic asylum.

There were scores of giggling and rather frightened nurses who screamed and scattered every time any kind of gun report was heard. The inmates had been moved out of hospital, and it was now filled to capacity with civilian casualties. Soon the blokes found out that I could talk to the civilians, and I was dragged from one group of nurses and paratroopers to another, translating. It was rather hard to tell who were the nurses and who were the inmates helping them. All were concerned to know where Prince Bernhard was and if their Queen had reached Dutch soil. They wanted to know which places had been liberated and if there would be any more bombing. It was quite a crazy atmosphere with our chaps, of course, trying to flirt and make up to them, being robbed of their cigarettes and sweets. The Dutch girls were bewildered by this onslaught and never far from tears and laughter, remembering again and again the hell they had gone through when they were being bombed the night before. Through some kind of misunderstanding, and probably due to my imperfect knowledge of their language, I was suddenly hailed as Prince Bernhard of the Netherlands and drawn into the hospital. I tried to explain, but it seemed to be quite useless in the confusion that followed the discovery. Only after I had been presented to the matron and given all my sweets and most of my cigarettes away, shaken hands with all the pathetic men, women and children who were lying injured in the hospital, was I allowed to resume my ordinary identity.

Our glider pilot flight officers now appeared and began to collect the flight. Burdened with our tremendously heavy rucksacks, we started moving off, cursing and swearing at having to leave our jeeps behind. In single file and directed by a parachute brigade officer we moved towards Arnhem. As the fire was getting heavier now our advance got slower and slower. We guessed that we were the tail of a

large column moving down towards Arnhem and were grateful for
the long halts, sometimes an hour or two at a time. It was impossible
to keep up with the paratroopers who only wore a very small pack.
This went on until two o'clock in the morning. We were making
less and less progress and heard an increasing volume of fire from
the direction of Arnhem. Eventually we got the order to turn round
and had to walk back half the way we had advanced that night. We
dug in along the railway line, covering the lane along which we had
advanced, to be ready for any attack that might come at dawn.

Tuesday

After a few hours the light came up and we went back to a wood near
our original RV point. We waited there for orders. At about 10 o'clock
fighters started passing overhead. We pointed them out to each other
and soon the usual argument started. 'They are Spits.' 'Don't be an ass,
anyone can see they are Typhoons.' 'Are they hell! Since when have
Typhoons got radial engines?' etc. I kept quiet, as usual when aircraft
recce is discussed, completely fascinated how anyone can be so clever
as to distinguish one fighter from another at any distance over 1000
feet. Even at that distance I can only tell a Spitfire and a non-Spitfire.
I was terribly pleased to be able to join the discussion effectively by
pointing out that they were German. This profound observation did
not bring me the credit I hoped for as everyone had seen the marking
at the same time. Before we had a chance to start a new argument as
to what type of German plane it was, their machine-guns fired at us.
We scattered and ran for shelter. Bullets were hitting ahead of us and
until some fools started firing at them with a Bren, they seemed to be
uncertain where our position was. The whole string of about fifteen
Focke-Wulf 190s and Messerschmitts turned about, losing height at
the same time. They had spotted us and for anyone who was not
in a slit-trench this was rather unpleasant. They raked us systematically, returning again and again. Once I had found a trench I had not

the slightest feeling of fear and realised how little damage this aerial machine-gunning could do. Our casualties were light and not one of our own Flight was hit.

We were told that it was our job now to clear the wood and hill of the enemy. Still burdened with our heavy rucksacks and all the equipment and food we had brought with us, we moved up the hill. The firing was becoming more and more intense; we could distinguish heavy and light machine-guns and all sorts of explosions. Of course we did not know whether they were ours or the enemy's, because most of us were under fire for the first time. We were told to spread out and go forward to the assault, crawling and hiding behind trees and bushes. At the moment there were only the odd bullets whistling over our heads, but still it was a hard job to keep in line, and the parachute officer had a hell of a time coaxing us forward in anything like a straight formation. Our two officers took the centre and I was the outside man on the left flank. We were about 30 all told.

I tried to work up enthusiasm and hatred for the kind of spirit which I thought was needed when assaulting the enemy. This was no doubt easier for me than for the others. I only had to think back a few years to the time when I was still a German. The past came back to me in flashes, and I had to remind myself that it had really happened, and to me … I was back in school … we had racial theory … the teacher called Hans to the front. He was the funny boy in our class, fat, short-sighted and clumsy, but always jolly, laughing and clowning. The teacher explained that Hans was a Jew and therefore harmful to the pure German stock which he polluted. Everyone laughed and made jokes, but I shall never forget the sight of Hans looking sad for the first time. I suddenly remembered that my father once told me that all my grandparents had been Jews. Should I not join Hans and tell them? But I did not. Perhaps it was that my courage failed me or maybe I did not have the presence of mind. Whenever I thought of it later I felt uncomfortable … which must have been guilt. Now I realised that this was my unique chance to make up for it to Hans and myself.

Another flash brought me back to the concentration camp. Subconsciously I looked at my hands. They had been bloody and festering from carrying heavy latrine buckets which I was forced to empty with my bare hands. I remembered my seventeenth birthday at Torgau concentration camp just about ten years ago. I was standing at the window of the dormitory unable to take my eyes off a group of bawling and laughing SA men below having their fun with an elderly Catholic priest by pushing him into the muddy pond where the pigs used to wallow. The priest was up to his shoulders in it, his hair and face were covered in muck so that he looked as if he were wearing a mask with openings only for eyes and mouth. Heavily and slowly he struggled through the thick slimy water towards the edge of the pond, but whenever he reached it the guards pushed him back. They took their time over it so that the whole thing seemed like a nightmare in slow motion. I remembered forcing myself to watch the ghastly spectacle until the priest had finally disappeared in the mud. I felt it was the only thing I could do. If I had not watched I might not have been able to believe it later on.

And I remembered the sickening picture of the smug and conceited SA and SS strutting the streets of my home town, Potsdam, as if they owned the world. I remembered how I used to dream of a most wonderful miracle by which these self-made Gods could be deprived of their uniform and power. Then all those who looked up to them would realise that they were the most ignorant and ridiculous bunch of people mankind had ever produced. The realisation that this was the glorious moment in which I could help this dream to come true gave me a feeling of incredible joy and elation. The circle had been completed, justice was being done ... and all this in my time. I was ready to take on anything and anybody that was German.

We reached the top of the hill and the fringe of the wood. In front of us was a large clearing with trees and branches only just felled. This clearing went level for about 200 yards and then dropped steeply and rose again. On the rise, where the brushwood and trees were still growing, were the Germans.

Loud German voices were heard, motor engines were running, and constant machine-gun and rifle fire was directed towards us. I halted a moment before advancing into the clearing to allow the centre and right flank to move up, and when I saw them coming I crawled forward. Bullets were whizzing about us from all directions, but there was no chance of finding out where they came from because the enemy's cover was too good. I found it impossible to advance any further with this damn rucksack on my back so I got rid of it. Looking round, I heard our Captain call desperately for our Lieutenant and I guessed that the centre of our advance must have had casualties. I was still feeling fighting mad and could not help crawling forward, firing rounds at any movement I could see in front of me. Dodd – one of the pilots of my flight – was on my right only about ten yards behind me and I shouted to him that I was going forward. Jerry's shouting and yelling was now quite clear; the firing at us seemed to be pretty inaccurate, but consistent. I felt I could not wait for the others. I got up and ran upright down the slope, fell behind cover, then up again and on. I vaguely noticed the intense fire, but all I wanted was to get there, and down I stumbled again between the branches and brushwood of the clearing. I waited and listened for any of our blokes, but all I could hear were terrific bursts of machine-gun fire and the Germans just in front of me. I could understand every word they were saying. Yet my mother tongue seemed like a foreign language to me, for, by the use of a new, overbearing and pompous vocabulary, plus a clipped military way of talking, the Nazis had deprived the German language of much of its sensitiveness and beauty. It sounded terribly ugly and repulsive.

They were quarrelling and swearing at each other. Now they were talking about me and an officer or NCO was telling them to go and search for me because someone had reported my presence. They would not obey, saying that they could not leave the clearing because of the strong enemy fire. Instead, they raked the ground all around me with a machine-gun and threw a few hand grenades. I crawled right under the brushwood and saw and heard the bullets splashing the ground and hitting the branches and tree stumps all round me. I was sure this was going to be the end and kicked myself for doing such an idiotic thing; trying to take a strong German position on my own. I swore that if ever I got out of this hopeless position I would never again be such a bloody fool. I lay completely still, bullets whizzing about me. I wondered if I wanted to pray; that is what everybody is supposed to do in a position like this; but I just did not feel like it, and to calm and steady myself I watched a colony of ants go about their well-planned and systematic business.

The Germans were arguing about me again. They did not want to go out to look for me, and so suggested that I must be dead. The more I listened to them, the more I realised what a badly disciplined and poor crowd they were and how easily we could have got them if we had only made a properly planned attack. They were talking now about leaving me until they got their heavier stuff there and I decided that I must at least try to get out of it. I edged back, but every time I moved, either the branches moved with me or my rifle got entangled. I had to do something drastic and quickly too, for now they knew I was alive. I threw a hand grenade to the left, dropped my rifle and ran for it. For the first few yards nothing much happened and all the firing seemed to go well away from me, but then it came nearer and nearer and I had to flop down. Lying in the brushwood I felt a curious restriction around my legs and discovered that my pants had somehow slipped down inside my trousers and that I could not possibly make another dash for it. There was nothing else to do but start the complicated business of cutting them in two separate parts. This done, I got up again and made one big dash for the top of the hill and the fringe of the wood from which we originally started our attack. They were still firing at me like mad from the Jerry lines, and now our chaps, who had retired into the wooded area, saw me coming towards them. They also opened up a concentrated fire upon me. Down I went again. I tried to shout, but the moment I moved they let go again and the noise was terrific. I tried again and again and nearly panicked. I just could not make them realise. How I wished that I had a recognition flag, but they were only issued to the first pilots of every crew. I gave up and lay behind the tree, not caring who shot me. It was a ridiculous situation. At last one of the parachute officers realised that something was wrong and stopped firing for a moment. He gave me a chance to call the password. They shouted to me to get up and raise my hands. Up I got. They went on firing, so I had to lie down again. It was only then I realised that I was still clutching a hand grenade; since I had abandoned my rifle this was my only weapon; I had forgotten all about it when I put up my hands. They shouted at me to put it down and fired again. Only after telling them exactly who I was, was I allowed to go forward.

I told the parachute officer about the bad morale of the Germans and that if he attacked now he would be sure to bowl them over. I said the same to the men who were near me and was asked to come with them into the new assault. I did not like this at all because I thought that it was tempting providence too far, but after encouraging them in this way I could hardly stay behind. So off I went again, to the fringe of the wood to take up an assault position. I vaguely heard engine noises from the German side, then a terrific crash and black smoke and sand flew up in the air; the Germans were using tanks or self-propelled guns. The second shot went straight into our line of attack and six men on the left flank were knocked out. There was nothing to do but retire to our original position, and I linked up with our flight, who were digging in on the rear slopes of the hill.

They told me that they had four casualties when we started our first attack, and that our Lieutenant was still out there in the brushwood seriously injured. I wanted to go back and look for him as I had seen something moving just when we were going in for the second attack, and I was certain that I could find him if he was still alive. Two of the blokes came with me and waited on the fringe of the wood whilst I searched the brushwood. I found him at last, but he was dead and it was not worth while getting the other chaps along to pull him out. We could definitely have had casualties doing so. Back to our old positions and digging in, we started making some tea and things as we had not had anything except biscuits, chocolate and sweets since Monday morning. Just before four o'clock the first bombers appeared on the horizon. They came slowly towards us in a seemingly never-ending stream. There were Stirlings, Halifaxes and Dakotas, many of them with gliders in tow. The whole sky above us was filled, like a moving ceiling, just below the cloud base. It was an awe-inspiring show of might; it seemed impossible that anything could deter this steadily advancing flow from its pre-determined route. The deep all-filling drone of their hundreds and hundreds of engines made you feel the spell even more. Then, as if by a single word of command, scores of ack-ack batteries opened up. The throb of the engines was suddenly swamped by the furious bark of the guns. The ear-splitting fury of the attack from the ground was indescribable. The stately procession of bombers carried on without seeming to take any notice for a few seconds; then these giants began lumbering out of the way, diving, banking, climbing. It seemed so undignified and pathetically clumsy, somehow. They were so helpless; I have never seen anything to illustrate the word 'helpless' more horribly. Now the sky was chaos: puffs of exploding shells, bombers alight, bombers plunging towards the earth, gliders casting off and banking steeply, and in between all this an irregular thick pattern of parachutes; men and supplies float-ing down. We of the first and second lifts thanked God that we were already on the ground.

But we never finished that meal, as the order came to move back to Wolfheze. Five minutes later we joined a stream of troops moving back slowly; we realised that this was a retreat. We were evacuating the woods and hills we had been about to dig into. It was a long stream of troops, of all units, walking rather quietly down the slope. Disorganisation started when we had to cross an open field which led to the railway lines. This field was under rather inaccurate German fire, but still it made everybody run. When we reached the other side we were not an organised body of men. The men had lost their officers and the officers their men. But everyone was disciplined and quiet in themselves, and there was no shouting or pushing. We helped each other along, said 'sorry'; we were just dazed and found the retreat rather incomprehensible.

We got to Wolfheze crossroads where troops were lining the road and bunching together everywhere. It was impossible to find out what the plan was and what we were going to do. I felt terribly uncomfortable as I knew the Germans were so near, and, disorganised as we were, we could not possibly put up any resistance. There were 20 of us, mostly from our own Flight, and as we could get no clear-cut information of what to do, I thought it best to retreat towards the river, where we hoped the Second Army would soon relieve us. I knew that it might be wrong to go on retreating off our own bat, but my feeling of uneasiness at remaining bunched together near the railway lines and crossroads was so strong that I could not do anything else.

We started using our compass and maps, and took a road which was supposed to lead to the river just right of Arnhem. It became very quiet the farther we got. We could hear distant firing, both of small arms and artillery from either side of the road, but we did not meet a soul. Most of the chaps felt that this was too uncertain and the silence depressed them. They said they would return to Wolfheze and I didn't argue as I did not want to be responsible for them. This move of mine was purely instinctive and there was no plan or reason attached to it. Only Dodd stayed with me, and we carried on along the lonely road. I never saw any of the people I left in Wolfheze again. They did not come away with us at the final pulling out of the First Airborne Division, so I do not know what happened to them, nor could any of the people I asked tell me. We walked on just inside the woods, never losing sight of the main road. Just as it was getting dusk a string of jeeps came racing along. We hailed them – it was a reconnaissance patrol and they were glad to take us as they had had some casualties and their numbers needed making up. We raced through the woods at 60 miles an hour, sitting sideways on the jeeps and covering the woods on either side with our guns. We were lucky and got right through to the Recce HQ without meeting any of the enemy. It was getting dark now and they were already dug in for the night, so all we had to do was to get some tins of food and blankets. Of course we had nothing at all, having had to leave our rucksacks behind, but the Recce blokes gave us plenty of everything, and we did not have to take turns on guard. I got myself a Sten-gun, plenty of filled mags and had a whole night's sleep in my slit-trench.

Wednesday

After breakfast they called for a patrol to push forward on to Arnhem railway bridge. Dodd and myself were asked to go. Off we raced again, and after ten minutes the first jeep encountered fire and pulled into the side. From here our advance was very slow. Everybody, except the driver, got out and worked their way forward on both sides of the road. On one side was a thick wood and on the other houses with gardens in front of them.

Progress was slow, now that the jeeps were parked in the gardens along the side streets, and two officers and twelve of us moved into the wood on the right. The others advanced through the gardens on the left. We heard German voices shouting and bawling just on the right of us, and also saw some of them moving backwards towards the bridge. We exchanged fire, but it was pretty inaccurate on both sides and we kept on, moving forward quite steadily. Then I heard the same engine noise as yesterday, and not long after the same old crash and thud. The tank was moving forward and firing shells into the houses across the road on our left. The chaps across the road stopped advancing and we manned a defensive position in the wood. We put a Piat gun in position and lay there waiting. The noise of the tank got nearer and nearer, and so did the shells hitting the houses opposite us.

A tank advancing firing shells is the most frightening think imaginable, and of all the experiences I had later on I was never more frightened than now. I believe that this is what makes a tank such a formidable weapon. We only had a little Piat gun just three feet long. The feeling of helplessness and fear became stronger and stronger the nearer the tank came. And at the same time the German infantry was working round us, obviously screening the tank. The voices and shouts seemed to be all about us. Just in front of us someone had thrown a smoke grenade on the road and, before we knew what had happened, the Recce had crossed the road. We saw them start up their jeeps and off they went. There was only the Piat gunner, his Number Two, Dodd and myself left. We decided to try and make our way back to the Recce HQ.

We could not cross the road any more as the tanks were firing down it like mad, but we knew that we had to cross it if we wanted to reach our destination. We withdrew through the wood parallel with the road, firing our guns to keep the Germans away, and throwing a hand grenade now and then to frighten them more than anything. Like that, we got as far as the crossroads which were about four miles from our HQ. Here there was no chance of crossing the road or of getting any farther, as we heard German voices from all directions.

There was nothing left but to hide and hope for the best. We were now in the back gardens of some houses near the crossroads. The two Recce blokes hid in a thicket just behind, while Dodd and I approached a house. We looked into a little shed and thought of going into the house and hiding in the cellar, but we did not know whether the civilians were Dutch Nazis or friendly. Just then we heard footsteps approaching. I spotted the rubbish dump belonging to the house – it was a little pit, four feet by two feet and about three feet deep, neatly hidden by some shrubs just about ten feet from the door. We crouched in it, and had just got our heads below the shrubs when the Germans came in to search the garden. They looked into the shed and through the house and, after satisfying themselves that none of us were hiding there, they just stood about talking in very loud voices and giving each other orders which no one obeyed. Most of the time they stood two or three feet from us. It was terrible in this dug-out. The decaying garbage stank and gradually seeped through our trousers. Our limbs got cramped and we felt pins and needles everywhere. There was no chance of moving at all, but the desire to move was irresistible. Then I discovered that my arms reached the sides of the trench and, by moving my hands, I could undercut the trench and so clear a little space for our feet. Dodd followed my example, and after an hour's scratching things became a little more bearable. After what seemed like ten years, the Jerries left the garden. We were just contemplating making a move when we saw a glider pilot jump out of the back door of one house and into the next. Oh, the agony when we tried to get out of our pit! But the joy of seeing a friend made us jump out of the pit and into the house.

The glider pilot told us that we must get away quickly. He had hidden in the attic of the house next door and from there had shot the whole crew of a tank that was standing on the corner of the crossroads. He had just got out of the house when they came to search it. Obviously they would search this one too. All three of us scrambled back through the garden to find the thicket where the two Recce blokes had hidden. They were still there and another six men besides. We crawled in and lay down exhausted, to wait for the night. It was only just afternoon, and it looked like being a pretty long wait. Very soon mortars and shells started whistling over us and the firing became more and more intense. We lay there, completely silent, on our stomachs, as near to the ground as possible. There was no chance of digging in or of taking shelter in this thicket surrounded by Germans. Lying there so inactive made us all desperately frightened. But we were lucky, for after about two hours the bombardment ceased, and we started whispering and making plans. A patrol of ten men approached us; their quiet and disciplined movements betrayed them straight away as British. It was Lieutenant W with ten glider pilots from different squadrons. He asked us all if we wished to join his little group and try to make our way back to the glider pilot HQ. We three were only too pleased. The Recce blokes preferred to stay in the woods until nightfall.

Fortunately Mr W knew the geography of this place quite well and, following his compass, led us through the woods. Again, long before we met the Germans, we were warned of their presence by their shouting and calling to each other. We took up a defensive formation, but carried on in the same direction. Then we came upon them about 100 yards in front of us. They were filing into an isolated house, surrounded by a wall, which was standing amidst the trees. We let go and several of them fell down injured. The others started rushing out from the house, colliding with the ones trying to get in. They were apparently helpless, and our two Bren-guns were just getting into position to let go into their midst, when I asked Mr W if he and the others could cover me. I got up and walked straight towards the Jerries, clutching my Sten-gun and feeling amazingly safe and powerful. I shouted 'Hande hoch!' and told them that the Second Army was just coming up, that they were hopelessly surrounded, and would they come and give themselves up. Very slowly they started filing out of the house into the road and I walked nearer; suddenly an officer appeared and furiously ordered them back.

We started firing and hit some of them. But they started to return our fire from the windows of the house, and of course, as there must have been about 50 of them inside, we could not hope to beat them now that the officer was organising the defence. We decided to withdraw. Unfortunately the young glider pilot, who had just before killed the whole crew of a tank single-handed, got shot in the stomach and Mr W detailed two chaps to take him back to our Divisional HQ whilst we kept Jerry busy in the house.

Eventually we reached a place on the outskirts of Arnhem called Oosterbeek. This was mostly occupied by our troops, and here were the Div. and Brigade HQs. It was to be our defence perimeter during the rest of the operation. It was glorious to see British troops again, and I went into the first house to refill my empty sten mags. They were making tea and of course that was heaven, and I had to remain and have a mess tin filled with some biscuits and jam. After I had loaded myself with food and ammunition I found I had lost Mr W. I asked my way to the Division HQ and from there got to the Glider Pilot Regiment.

There were quite a few of them dug-in in a large park. They were guarding the Div. HQ, which was a very massive hotel [the Hartenstein] surrounded by large outbuildings, hothouses, etc. I think the place had been very famous. Until a few days previously it had harboured the German HQ for this area. There were not many people I knew in the trenches, as they came from different squadrons, but as there was no sign of anyone from my own flight, I decided to remain with them. I was much too tired to go round looking, and anyhow what did it matter where one fought? They were all living in extremely deep slit-trenches with roofs and branches and all sorts of ingenious contraptions covering them. I heard that I had arrived during the third lull that they had had. The mortar fire was increasing all the time, and I had to find myself a slit-trench for the night. Eventually I did find six blokes of my flight, but none of them had heard anything of the rest of the flight or of our officers. I joined them, and one of the pilots offered to share his slit-trench with me as it was too late to dig one of my own. I also met Vic Wade, who was my best friend back at the station, and several others. I felt that I could not possibly spend the night in the trench with Jimmy Plant as there was not room for two, so I moved a bed out of the gardener's house, which was just behind us and very badly knocked about. I put it right next to the trench and slept comfortably in sheets on a feather bed.

For some reason or another that night the mortaring was rather light and mainly on the far side of the perimeter. Or maybe I slept so deeply that I was not aware of the danger. But not once during the night did I have to roll out of bed into the trench.

Thursday

After the dawn stand-to, we were just getting breakfast ready, which
meant heating the prepared tins of bacon, beans, steak and kidney
pie or anything which we could scrounge, when the most intense
mortaring of the Division HQ started. It was our area which took
the brunt of this attack and everyone crouched in the trenches. It
was quite terrifying. Any kind of danger is a hundred times more
frightening when one has to remain inactive, and all we could do
was to crouch in our trenches, feeling the mortar fire creep nearer
and nearer. Someone who could not reach his own trench in time
jumped in on top of Jimmy Plant and myself but we did not dare to
move as the hits were falling right amongst us. There was a thunder-
ous crash … the walls of the trench crumbled and we were covered
with branches and sand – I felt dazed and was certain that my ear-
drums must have burst. We kept still for several minutes, just to make
sure that we were all in one piece and asked each other if we were
all right. Then we clambered out and found that nothing had happened to us. The crater was just an arm's length from our trench and
I could touch the centre from where I stood. The mortar had gone
right through the centre from where I stood. The mortar had gone
right through my beautiful bed and shot it back through the window
into the house. There was no more breakfast for any of us – not that
we would have been able to eat any. The barrage passed on towards
the Division HQ building. An officer asked for volunteers to go on a
patrol. I was glad to get out of this, and off we went through the park
and the perimeter.

The main road passed along one side of our perimeter and was
crossed by another road which formed the other border of our position. This smaller road had a row of houses along its left side, which
led away from the perimeter; on the right side of the road was a wood
with a few houses standing in the trees. At the back of the houses on
the left-hand side was a vegetable plantation 200 yards wide, belong-

ing jointly to this row of houses and the row opposite, making a
large square which was surrounded on three sides by the backs of
the houses. There were about 20 small plots and gardens with fruit
trees, runner beans and all sorts of vegetables. We advanced through
these gardens to find out if they houses on both sides were occupied.
This was a very slow and laborious undertaking. We crawled towards
a house, waited and listened, crawled again, waited, and so on and so
on. As we didn't seem to make any headway, I began to get impatient.
I got up, went to the next house, knocked on the door, went in and
shouted 'Jemand hier?' (Anyone at home?) and as there wasn't, we
went through the rooms to make sure. This went on admirably from
house to house, and speeded up operations considerably. In one house,
some civilians answered my call and led me to a cellar where there
was a wounded British paratrooper. We sent someone back to fetch
a medical orderly. We made sure of all the buildings along the cab-
bage patch and crossed over the road at the far side of the plantation,
which ran parallel to the main road, where my polite enquiry resulted
in a stampede – not towards us, but away from us, Jerry, apparently did
not care for visitors, and made his exit, leaving a machine-gun and
various other equipment. There seemed to be about six of them, who
bolted into the house opposite. We lobbed hand grenades after them
before they could take cover, and one of them was laid out. I had run
upstairs and could see them inside a trench and behind hedges, trying
to crawl away. I fired, and hit another, then went on lobbing hand
grenades from my position overlooking their trench. Captain Z sent
me along the road to try to link up with a party which the Colonel
had led, to report Jerry's position, it was a pity we couldn't drive them
out of more of the houses, but we were not supposed to get into a
serious fight. We had to await orders.

So we remained in one house and were told later to retire back
into the vegetable plantation and occupy the houses on the right. The
row on the other side was to be occupied by the KOSB (King's Own
Scottish Borderers). We split our own party into two and took over

the corner house at the far end of the street and the corner house on the large road nearest to our defence perimeter. We stayed in this street until the whole Division withdrew on the Monday. Our position was in the lower corner house. The CO of our party was a big young man with a fair, stately moustache [this was Captain Ogilvie]. He wore a kilt. With him, there were five other officers and about 50 other glider pilots. The end house was occupied by two officers and about ten to fifteen men. The moment we moved in, Jerry started to harass us. Apparently he had had the same idea, just a bit too late. He was now sniping at us from the woods and the few houses which faced the road opposite our row. We could not walk from one house to another, or appear in any of the front rooms, without someone having a pot at us.

We started to settle down in our two houses; digging trenches in the front garden and setting up Bren-gun positions which would cover as much of the road as possible, but we were too many in each house and much too disorganised, and there were only a few hours of daylight left. No one did anything about barricading the front windows and occupying the twelve houses and gardens which lay between us. I felt that something must be done very quickly if we were going to survive that night, for Jerry was becoming more and more active in the wood only 20 yards away. Everyone was clustering together in the two houses and nothing was being done. I went to see Captain Z and, with the help of a lieutenant and others, we worked out a plan to occupy at least every second house until we got enough reinforcements to defend every house in the street. Many of the things I had read in descriptions of street fighting in Spain came back to me and they proved invaluable later on. We barricaded the front windows so that Jerry could not throw hand grenades into them. We dug communication trenches from one house to another and chiselled holes in brick walls. We put up branches for cover and did everything possible to have safe, invisible communications along the whole street.

Our main idea was that, if any house could not hold out, the occupants could fall back upon the next house and reinforce it; besides, it was essential to know what was going on in every part of our street.

That night I stayed in the lower corner house, firing magazine after magazine up the road with our Bren-gun to prevent Jerry crossing over from the wood. They fired back fiercely all night but did not dare to attack us. As soon as the first light came we went on with our preparations, and also got some reinforcements from the Div. HQ. In addition, some of the Polish Parachute Brigade, which had landed on the other side of the river and fought its way over, were detailed to our street. They took up positions in three houses in the middle of the row. We glider pilots could not concentrate in the top six houses. It was a relief after having the responsibility of the whole street on our shoulders, especially as we had had several casualties during the night. There was not a day when a few of us weren't knocked out. Our Glider Pilot HQ was in the third house from the top, and there were ten of us holding it. The street was not completely occupied.

Friday

During the morning the first German SP gun started moving around the top crossroad. We heard the engine revving and the Jerries shouting before the attack started.

The immediate job was to put our Piat gun in a position where it could dominate the road and prevent the SP gun from moving down. We found an ideal place which Jerry never spotted the whole time we were there. We decided to fire the bomb through a little hole in the roof of the attic. The noise of the tank got louder. We could hear the tracks squeaking and grinding along the road. Then the first shots were fired and tore away some bricks from the front of the houses. From the wood opposite came the splutter of a heavy Spandau machine-gun and a hail of light machine-gun and rifle bullets came across the road. Jerry was also using small armour-piercing shells, which could penetrate clean through a house. This was all preparation for the SP. Until we could see the tank coming, we used the Bren-gun from our high look-out and sprayed the crossroads and the wood opposite us with continuous fire. Germans were moving about, unaware that they could be seen, and many of our bullets found their mark. Lieutenant X came up to the attic and offered to fire the Piat gun. He had just a little more experience with it than I had, as he had once fire a practice shot while I had once been shown how to load it. A wave of disgust rose in me against those petty-minded officers and sergeant-majors who had wasted weeks, even months, with drill and kit inspection, making us lay out our boots, tooth-brushes, knives, forks and other kit, as per regulation. Why couldn't they have taught us about house-to-house fighting and the Piat gun? But then, drill, and lining up of beds and blankets, occupies the greatest number of men with the least effort.

Lieutenant X waited until we could see the tank clearly – it could not have been more than 100 yards from us. Then he fired the first round. It was the greatest joy I had felt for a long time when we heard and saw the terrific explosion this little weapon produced, a relief which could hardly be described.

To sit there waiting for the monster needed all our patience and strength for we had no idea what this little apparatus could do against it. Lieutenant X was covered with dust and thrown against the other wall by the recoil as the bomb left the Piat. I had taken position next to him ready to jump forward and look through the hole to see where it hit. The direction was perfect, but it fell about 20 yards short. The SP stopped immediately and, by the time Lieutenant X had shaken himself and got back into position, I had reloaded. We fired another four or five shots, and the Jerries obviously couldn't decide whether it was one of our very few anti-tank guns or what, nor where it came from. They were firing straight ahead and at our side of the street, but all the shells went well past us, hitting houses and trees farther down. Apparently they hadn't the faintest idea that we were only 100 yards away, sitting with our pop-gun in the attic of the nearest house.

The SP retired about 50 yards, far enough to be out of our range. Now that we knew the value of our Piat we took it down into our safest back room, together with the bombs, and I continued firing the Bren-gun through the hole in the roof to cover the crossroads and make it hot for any Jerry who tried to cross into the woods opposite.

The firing and sniping went on. Suddenly it got quiet and, from our three hospital buildings on the lower crossroads just outside our perimeter, appeared two of our jeeps with large Red Cross flags. Whatever I personally felt about the Germans, I must give them their due; in this Arnhem action they couldn't have kept more strictly to the Geneva Convention, and this was confirmed by everyone I talked to. In a way their behaviour was so deliberate and precise that there must have been a policy behind it. Not once did I hear of any Red Cross men or jeeps being deliberately fired on, even when they appeared on the most contested road in the midst of the heaviest fighting. There were several men I spoke to who were taken prisoner by fast-advancing tanks and whom Jerry allowed to go back to our lines with a kind of slap on the back. The work of the Red Cross personnel was wonderful. Tremendous courage and self-sacrifice is necessary to drive or walk out of hospital gates and along a road which is under fire from excited and heated troops. I was told that the casualties of the Red Cross were at least as heavy as those of the fighting men. It is difficult to see from 300 yards ahead if a man has a Red Cross armlet. Very often they couldn't be seen through our camouflage. Shooting at them by the Germans, or even by our own men, could not possibly be avoided.

The casualties in the lower houses of our street must have been very heavy as the jeeps soon reappeared with their stretchers occupied and wounded with first-aid bandages sitting on the sides. Other wounded were walking behind a Red Cross flag carried by one of the orderlies.

The firing started up the moment the Red Cross party disappeared into our lines and stopped the moment they came out again.

I left my post for a minute to get some rest. I wanted to see how our house had stood up to the attack and whether there had been any casualties. The situation seemed to be well in hand and we were still in possession of the corner house, though the tank had been more or less level with it when we had stopped it. The occupants told us of the relief they had felt when they saw the first Piat bomb hit the road. They thought we had damaged one of the tracks, as the SP retired in jerks as if it was out of control; it might even have been pulled back by a recovery tractor. Everyone reported that the sniping and firing was very bad, and we decided that our communications between the houses must be improved. We needed deeper and longer trenches, camouflaged with branches, to allow us to dig in comparative safety.

Three of us went round systematically barricading our front windows and doors. We saw the effect of hand grenades in the front rooms. Barricading was an uncomfortable job; we had to use the beautiful antique furniture, which must have been of great value, to block up the windows and doors. All this stuff was going to be wrecked at the next attack. The front rooms and facades of the houses suffered each time. This job of barricading had to be redone every time we had a respite, though we never had a real respite as rifle and machine-gun sniping kept on consistently and perseveringly.

One got skilled in avoiding being hit, and as time went on our casualties became fewer, though we were desperately tired and thought less about personal danger. But we had acquired a kind of sixth sense and somehow did the right things automatically. In moments of half-dozing, whilst manning my attic position, I felt terribly pleased and grateful for this newly discovered ability. No one can know beforehand or can influence his reactions to great personal danger. And this feeling of pride and pleasure compensated a little for the hatefulness of the whole bloody business. I hate war. I can't stop thinking of the friends and relatives of anyone who has been hit. I know the Germans. I have seen them do the most vile and frightful things. I know that they have destroyed millions of Jews and political opponents. But I do not enjoy killing or wounding anyone. Once I'm forced to fight, however, the whole affair becomes a matter of skill and a job that needs all my powers of concentration. I no longer consider the effect it has on my opponent.

We spent the rest of the morning watching carefully, trying to keep the snipers quiet and improving our position. Soon we began to feel very hungry and the food problem had to be seriously considered. I joined Graham in search of food. We hadn't had a single issue since we had landed. Most of us had lost our rucksacks, and those who had managed to save theirs had shared all their supplies. We were very lucky to find large stores of tinned food and provisions in the houses. I didn't know how the fellows managed who had to fight in the wooded country and fields, but we in the houses did very well. With a little bit of searching, we got the most magnificent meals together; these would have gone down well even at home. Every Dutch house has a store of food-preserves in all sorts of glass and earthenware containers. Trust the Dutch! In other houses they were all helping themselves liberally to bottled tomatoes, French beans and other vegetables, avoiding the preserves which had an unappetising look. I went round all the cellars, asking if I could take a few preserves with me. Our expandable battle smock could harbour at least three or four of the 'unappetising' preserves, and in my hand I carried a respectable jar. The first time I came back with my spoil there was a general outcry and I was told I would have to cook and eat it myself. I had the utmost difficulty in persuading some of the chaps to eat what they called 'Continental concoctions' but I finally did persuade them that, although they looked like bottled medical specimens, they were really very good to eat. As indeed they were.

Very soon everyone was eating like mad and had completely forgotten the war, the Second Army and the Jerry tanks. They were stuffing themselves with fried chicken, tenderloin of pork and beefsteak. We laid a fire with bricks in the middle of the kitchen floor. By this time everyone was enthusiastic about the food and was 'digging for victory' at the risk of their lives, in the plantation. This resulted in a flare-up of German fire as they thought we were going to launch an attack. All our rich harvest was thrown into a large slop pail and cooked on the open fire. It was delicious.

We felt like a rest, but the now-familiar though still ghastly sound of engines and tracks was heard again. Up dashed Lieutenant X to our beloved Piat gun and, loaded with bombs, I followed him to our attic position. With the aid of binoculars, we could just see a mass of branches and trees with movement behind it. We let go with a spray of Bren bullets to make it hot for any troops who might be hiding behind the tank or whatever was at the back of the approaching foliage. Now we knew that a lot of bullets and noise whizzing round Jerry, even if they were very inaccurate, would help us, and would discourage him from any personal assault or attack. He was desperately afraid of us, and that was one of the reasons why we held out until our planned withdrawal; that and our faith in the Second Army. There were so many proofs of this fear that there could be no doubt about it. First, when I was lying in front of the German lines and they did not dare advance or attack until their tank came. Again, when against ten of us nearly 50 of them in a strong position almost gave themselves up and were only stopped by an officer. Then, their constant shouting and bawling at night, for no other reason than to give themselves confidence. Also I had an opportunity to interpret for a Parachute Major, who did the preliminary interrogation of two German prisoners as soon as they were marched in.

They belonged to the SS Panzer Grenadiers and gave us their regiment and number of unit, etc. They said they had been in the army for six weeks and this was their first action. They were both about 40, and obviously had no intention of fighting anyone or for anything. They said that they knew the war was lost for Germany, and when I asked them why they fought us, when it was useless, they said that they had no choice and would have been shot by their own people at the slightest sign of refusal. I heard this sort of report over and over again.

If there had not been a sprinkling of first-class and fanatical officers and NCOs in this division, no fight would have been possible.
But even with the present state of affairs, it was ridiculous that they
did not wipe us out within a few hours. This Panzer division, with
tanks, mobile guns, flame-throwers, very close Focke-Wulf support
and the heaviest and most concentrated ack-ack seen by any of the
RAF pilots whom I met later on at the 'drome, and even mobile
loudspeakers with trained German propagandists spouting in English,
never dared to change over to direct assult or succeeded in penetrat-
ing our perimeter. No body of men, with only small arms as we had,
could possibly have withstood a German Panzer of the old material.

Slowly the mass of foliage drew nearer and started to fire down the
street at the lower houses. We could now see the immense tracks and
from their size we thought that this was probably a self-propelled gun.
We couldn't do anything for quite a long time, and even decided that
it would be inadvisable to go on firing the Bren, as this might give
our Piat position away. Only when the SP had got to within about
100 yards of us could we be active, and that would be a God-sent
relief. Waiting and watching the gun approach was almost unbearable.
It made a terrific noise and smoke each time it fired, and we could
hear the clatter of glass and masonry whenever one of the shells hit a
façade down the street.

We had decided that we must try and increase the range of our
bomb by elevating the Piat still further, using it more or less like a
mortar. Just in front of our attic were the branches of a large tree, and
about a couple of yards away was the corner of the next house. Our
first attempt proved pretty inaccurate, and the bomb must have hit
one of the tree branches and been diverted on to the corner of the
house next door where it exploded with a terrific blast. This really
shook us badly, though mainly Lieutenant X who was standing right
behind the Piat; he was flung against the back wall of the attic, and I
saw him covered with dust and looking very pale, crawling towards
the stairs. There was nothing seriously wrong with him, thank God,

it was just the effect of the blast that had winded and concussed him; for the moment he didn't seem to know what had happened. He went off down the stairs, and I continued firing bomb after bomb the old well-tried way. I yelled for someone downstairs to bring up more bombs and insert the fuses.

Well, we had done it again … I don't know how much we had damaged the SP, but it stopped firing and withdrew out of range, slowly and critically. It stopped just behind the rise in the street, and I could still see it from the top of our house, but the Jerries must have thought that any kind of anti-tank gun firing from the bottom corner couldn't see it. Men started busying themselves round it, until all the top houses opened up with their Stens, Brens and rifles and drove them out of sight.

As usual, after any kind of concentrated attack, the firing suddenly ceased when the Jerries, and we alike, brought out our ambulances to collect the wounded. Now that it was quiet, the old background of rumbling artillery was audible. We never knew whether this was ours or the Germans', but liked to think it was the Second Army shelling the German rear. There were always the rapid mortar explosions, falling mainly on the perimeter and Div. HQ, and bursts of machine-gun and small-arms fire, but these noises were so continuous through all the days and nights that we held this street that after a while we didn't hear anything, and everything seemed perfectly normal.

We were always busy at our posts, in the trenches in front of the houses, in the attics, at the windows, and in little firing positions made by removing a brick from the outside wall. We covered all the approaches in the gardens, the street or the woods. Reliefs were fixed mostly by mutual arrangement. Food was collected and cooked in the lull between the heavy arms attacks and attempted assaults. We were now busy again patching up all the breaches in the barricades round our house. They had to be complete for the night, and everyone felt much more confident about holding out than we had done the previous night.

By now Lieutenant X had recovered from his shock, and we visited other houses, making arrangements. He suggested an hour or two's nap before the inevitable intensification of activity on both sides at dusk. We went into the only still completely furnished room, called 'The Officers' Room' because in it, Captain Z, the CO, who had been wounded in the arm, was usually lying in a luxuriously heavy Continental bed, with sheets and pillow-case, covered with a quilted eiderdown. He lay fully dressed in kilt, sporran, boots and beret. Full of confidence and optimism, he received everyone on his bed, and it was difficult to know how far he realised the danger of our position. In addition to Captain Z there were usually a few other officers – men from the other houses, making plans and decisions in a nonchalant way.

Only once during the whole action did I hear any one of the officers really lose his temper, and that was when trying to wake up the Sergeant-Major, who had his HQ under the best table. It took me several visits to the Officers' Room to discover him, since the huge lace tablecloth, which overhung a purple velvet cover, hid him rather effectively. And that was exactly what the Sergeant-Major wanted. His aggressive nature on the parade-ground and in the barracks had changed entirely and he did not want people to notice. Everybody did, of course, know about it, but nobody could do anything, and in any case, there were plenty of us who could do his job.

Nobody could escape the spell of this room. The shutters were closed, and the candlelight, bed, couch and easy chairs gave it such a homely atmosphere. It needed great will-power to leave this room and carry on with any job. But at least it made you feel that somewhere there was still peace and homeliness. Lieutenant X and I had our nap on some cushions on the floor in a position that was safe against sniping or blast.

It was now dusk and everyone was mobilised for the stand-to. The supper was simmering in the pail and the chaps came down, as each was relieved, to have a plate of hot stew and some delicious preserved-fruit, with sweet condensed milk – the winter rations of the Dutch people. I was having my supper when Lieutenant X came into the kitchen and said would I come to the Officers' Room. I took my plate and went in. Captain Z had just seen the Brigadier and our own Colonel [Brigadier Hackett and Colonel Murray], and had been asked to send patrols out to discover the assembly point of the German armour, which was harassing our section, and to find out which of the houses at the end of our street opposite the top corner house were occupied by Germans. They asked me if I would like the job and how I would tackle it. I thought it best to take as few people with me as possible as the important thing was to get near Jerry undetected, one chap to be with me the whole time, and a small group waiting on the other fringe of the plantation where I would cross into Jerryland, to give me covering fire in case I should run into trouble and have to withdraw quickly.

I now had to find someone to come with me and I thought immediately of Sergeant Graham. He had taken a lot of pains and responsibilities far above his rank and seemed more or less to have the same ideas about the situation as I had. I brought him into the Officers' Room and we discussed our plan. We were going out on three patrols at 10, 12 and 2 o'clock, on three different points of the plantation. Next we had to go searching for civvy shoes or running shoes, and clean our Sten-guns and ammo. We slept until half-past nine, when we were supposed to meet our covering party, which Mr T [an officer] had offered to supply from his corner house. We never met his party. I don't know what happened or where it waited for us, but we were much too impatient to go searching for it and stumbling about, giving away our position and intentions. We crossed the plantation over the street to the next block of houses – slowly tip-toeing in the shadow of the houses. Sergeant Graham stayed about 20 yards behind me, following up every time I stopped for any length of time. German voices became audible now and we could hear engines running. They seemed to be manoeuvring their transport and armour.

Then we heard Germans walking through gardens. We lay just where we were. We began to distinguish a general movement from right to left. The German transport was moving to a point about a mile away, screened by small detachments moving parallel to them. We tried to get nearer the machines, but unfortunately we ran into a body of the enemy who immediately opened up on us, even though I'm sure they couldn't have seen us. We decided that we had better withdraw this time and try to get farther on our next patrol. We now had some idea of the lie of the land up to where we had to withdraw; that would save us a lot of time at 12 o'clock. Besides, we were supposed to cross into our own lines at half-past ten as our men had been given that time for our return and told to hold their fire. Now for a sleep, and by 12 o'clock we were ready once more. The troops covering the lines we had to cross were warned. We had realised that we must have longer for this patrol, so our time limit to get back was extended from 12 to 1.30.

We crossed over as quietly as possible and worked our way through the maze of the back gardens, among outhouses, shrubs and orchards. Soon we had passed far beyond the place where we had met the German patrol before; the talking was more distant now. We made slow and very careful progress. It was pretty nerve-racking, worming our way along, silently stopping every few minutes to listen for German footsteps and noises, which were to be heard now at much longer intervals. We could hear a more or less continuous noise of spades digging, and this was the direction we took. The noise led us to a thick clipped hedge, and we tried to wriggle through, but we got stuck again and again by our Sten-guns and things catching in the dense undergrowth. Then we found a square tunnel cut right underneath the hedge, through which we crawled. We emerged into a large open space, bounded on one side by the hedge and on the other by what looked like the outbuildings of a big country house. In the middle of the space were two immense oak trees with circular benches round their boles. A path ran up for about 100 feet, and at the top we saw the silhouettes of two Germans digging and whisper-ing monotonously. They looked quite unreal, as if they were standing on the walls of some fairy castle. This hill was not marked on any of our maps, and we had had no knowledge of its existence.

Here, obviously, was the German strong-point. From it they sent out troops and vehicles to dominate our position from the woods and houses opposite. We now realised that they occupied these houses and the wood during the daytime and withdrew their men and vehi-cles into this strong-point at night. At the moment it looked much more like a fairy castle. Graham though it would be a good idea to kill the two Jerries up there. They were less than 100 yards away. But our withdrawal through the gardens and orchards was going to be difficult in any case, and from their dominating position they would be able to plaster us with hand grenades, so I thought it not worth the risk as our information might be of great importance.

When we got back we were surprised to find it was well after two. We were glad to think that we now had a good excuse not to go on the third patrol. We got through our own lines without being accosted; either everyone was fast asleep, or perhaps they were waiting for us.

In our cosy Officers' Room we were surprised and rather touched to find that they hadn't all completely passed out, but were really quite anxious about us and our long stay.

Under normal conditions our report would have been of immense value, for now we could pinpoint the German position accurately on a map for artillery and mortar fire. But then we realised that, as we had not mortars or artillery, there was nothing we could do about it, although it was interesting from a military point of view. It was valuable, however, to know that Jerry left his houses every night and retired to safe, prepared positions. Obviously the men refused to spend the night so near the British lines. That was a compliment. If only we'd had the men, we could have given the Germans a lovely surprise by infiltrating into their houses and establishing ourselves there by dawn. Still, Captain Z must have been pleased, and attached quite a bit of importance to our report, for he condescended to sit up in bed, twirl his handsome moustache, and say, 'Well done, chaps. Good show. You've got to see the Brigadier tomorrow …' Graham and I gathered up some cushions and blankets from the floor, found a corner and passed out until stand-to at dawn.

Saturday

It was rather quieter the next morning, and we all felt in a more domestic mood. We cleared up some of the mess in the kitchen; this was indescribable, though obviously unavoidable. We fished hand grenade fuses out of bottled cherries and disentangled small arms and ammunition from the vegetable store. From a pump in one of the back gardens that was not too exposed to sniping we collected water for the day. I did a bit of gardening, which consisted of crawling into the plantation with a sack which I filled with potatoes, tomatoes, sweet corn, fruit and anything handy. In each house there was a large neat stack of onions, and these in themselves made every meal wonderfully tasty.

We had our regular slop-pail stew again. We never got tired of this, there was such a wonderful variety of ingredients. No one ever quite knew what he was eating, as anyone who had collected something just threw it in the pail. Buckley, the only private in our section, slowly developed the job of cook. He resented being asked to cook or being called cook, however, as his real job was that of batman, and he felt he had come down in the world, but when we addressed him like this we meant it as a compliment.

This morning there was even some talk about washing and shaving, but that was going a bit too far as the firing was increasing again and positions had to be carefully manned. Lots of the chaps were pretty sorry sights in the morning after all night in the trenches or firing positions. They had to sit staring into the dark shivering, and worst of all, fighting the irresistible desire to sleep, when they had had hardly any rest at all. Graham and I thought the subsequent session in the cosy Officers' Room was well worth a little patrol every night.

All the men in this sector consisted of senior NCOs who were pilots, like the officers. Such different and separate jobs as officers and men have in the ordinary army did not exist to the same extent in our outfit. We all got on splendidly together and, although we lived for eight days in the most intimate relationship, I never once heard an NCO drop the 'Sir' when addressing an officer. It must be remembered that our present position was unnaturally difficult and somewhat removed from the role we are usually called upon to play on these operations.

If this had not been the case, these pilot officers might never have been tested in leadership and improvisation. The power to improvise and act quickly, in completely unforeseen circumstances, only comes to the fore when the occasion arises.

Only on this comparatively quiet morning did we realise that we were not the only occupants of these houses in the front line. Pale, quiet, frightened people appeared from the cellars. They inquired timidly where they could get some water, and if it would be possible for them to venture into the house proper to collect some blankets and food. There were something like ten people in each cellar, and I went down to see if I could help them, as I was the only one who could make himself understood. I spent the greater part of the morning being asked to various houses to translate their wants and difficulties, although quite a few of them spoke English.

In our house there had lived, unnoticed until now, a grandfather, father, mother and three children, besides some other people who had moved down from a devastated house. None of them complained, and they seemed to be quite apathetic to the destruction of their beautiful houses and furniture.

There appeared to have been a great many Dutch fifth columnists in this area. Most of them were members of the Dutch National Socialist Party, working in the closest co-operation with the Germans, and, in most cases, favouring the total incorporation of their country. The next house to ours belonged to one of these collaborators. The husband had fled with the Germans the moment the first glider appeared in the sky, but the wife and daughter were still in the cellar. The wife had given birth to a boy on the first night of the British occupation. In the rooms of this house we found many photographs of German officers, arm in arm with Dutch girls in uniform, giving the Hitler salute. There was also a gold-framed picture of the owner of the house shaking hands with the Gauleiter. It seemed that the daughter had made friends with some German girls and was carrying on the most idiotic correspondence with them.

We found many German magazines and publications, the weekly war reports were superbly produced; better than anything I have seen here or even from the USA. They really brought the war to the reader – the personal hardships and difficulties of the troops, the supply problems and the strategy. Reading them, it was quite impossible to imagine how Germany could ever lose the war. These publications even impressed us, so their impact on the Germans must have been immense. We got a good laugh, seeing these heroes in print and photograph, when we thought of our personal contact with them.

My study of the German magazines in the Dutch Nazi's house was cut short, as Captain Z and Lieutenant X wanted to take me with them to see the Brigadier at Division HQ to report on our patrol of the night before. We kept to the backs of the houses, worming our way from one garden to another. This was not nearly as easy as it should have been, as two of the houses in the row were now occupied by men of the Polish Parachute Brigade, who had come to relieve us the night before. It seemed that these men took war very seriously; and, from reports that had come to us during the night and this morning, great caution had to be exercised whenever we came anywhere near the vicinity of their lines. Captain Z, Lieutenant X and I thought it the best policy to approach them upright and rather noisily. We started talking at the top of our voices and got right into their trench, optimistically thinking we were past the danger, when we were halted by a pair of flashing eyes glaring at us over the top of a rifle. Some sound, which might have been a challenge but was more like a war cry, blared at us from only a yard away, and for the moment we couldn't quite decide what to shout back. Then Lieutenant X managed to think of the password, but it had no effect. The gun was still pointed at us and even Captain Z's hearty 'Don't be a bloody, fool, man!' met with no response at all. It occurred to me that perhaps the kilts worn by the two officers might have put this fierce warrior on the wrong track, so I pushed forward and told him quietly that we wanted to get to Div. HQ. Then I tried in German, but he didn't even notice the difference in the two languages. Thank God, one of their officers appeared before the worst could happen. By this time we were in quite a state and Captain Z asked for a Polish guide before we continued our short journey through their lines. Our progress was desperately slow, for whenever we reached another Polish trench or firing position a long and animated argument opened up between our guide and his 'opponent'. Several times we thought we should have to interfere between the two to avert bloodshed. But I suppose it was really only a series of friendly chats between tough guys.

When we got to the large main road, which was under both German and our own fire, it was comparatively easy after what we had just been through. To cross into the perimeter we had to make a dash for it one after the other. Our own trenches were manned and we were greeted in a friendly tongue. They directed us to the Division HQ and to the part where the Brigadier was supposed to be at the moment. It was not, as you might think, a respite when we arrived there. The continuous rain of mortars had increased since the morning when I left on patrol and never came back. Everybody who was not working in the cellars of the big house was living and working in very deep, narrow slit-trenches; they looked rather tired and harassed. The mortaring was very uncomfortable and was taking a steady toll of these defenceless people, pinned down as they were.

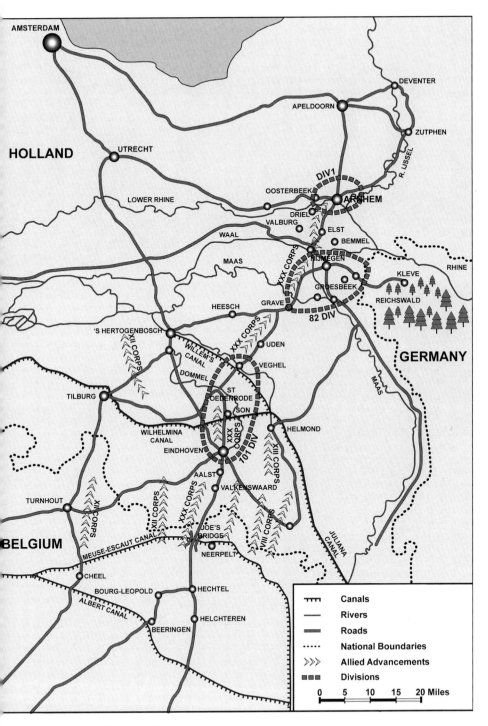

The plan for Operation *Market Garden*, September 1944.

Louis (second from left) in the Pioneer Corps, 1940.

Louis in flying kit, 1944.

Winrich Behr at La Roche Guyon,
spring 1944.

Winrich Behr with
Field-Marshal Rommel,
Normandy, February
1944.

Sergeant Louis Hagen (left), Glider Pilot Regiment, with his two brothers, 1944.

The air armada for *Market Garden* deployed the two American and one British airborne divisions. Photographed here are four gliders in the Landing Zone.

jor General 'Boy' Browning in October 1942 when commanding 1st Airborne Division. By tember 1944 he was commander of I British Airborne Corps. (IWM H.24128)

ding Zone 'S' on the first day, with Horsas dropping men and equipment.

C47s dropping men and supply canisters over the DZ.

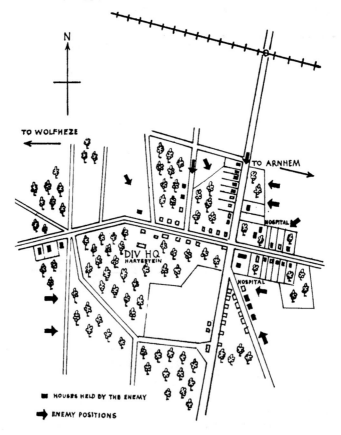

N

TO WOLFHEZE

TO ARNHEM

DIV HQ
HARTESTEIN

HOSPITAL

HOSPITAL

■ HOUSES HELD BY THE ENEMY

➡ ENEMY POSITIONS

Where Louis went into action.

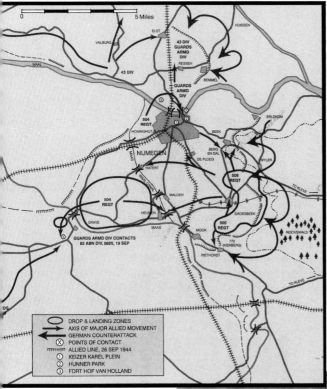

German counterattacks
against the 82nd Airborne
Division and XXX Corps.

September, just to the east of
Arnhem road bridge; three
n of the 1st Parachute Squadron,
 – Sapper C. Grier (left), Lance
rporal R. Robb (right) and Sapper
Dunney (background) – have just
come prisoners of war. (IWM
J.2131)

Winrich Behr in 1983.

Louis Hagen in later
life.

The nervous strain of it was mirrored in their drawn white faces and unsteady eyes. These, I felt, were the real heroes of Arnhem. It looked very brave to volunteer for patrol and to defend a day position like our row of houses ... but I knew full well that it was not dare-devilishness, hate of the Germans or a sense of duty that made me volunteer so readily for the first patrol on Thursday ... but the simple fact that I was afraid of being frightened by the slow rain of mortars.

I soon found that others might have fared better had they acted as I did. Not all had stood up to the strain. In the darkest part of the cellar in the HQ, and in a storage room deep below the gardener's cottage, I found men who had lost all their nerve and self-control. They looked like people who had been seasick for days. Nothing in the world could coax them up. Down there they vegetated; they ate, slept and relieved themselves, in a world where only their fear was reality. They were men, and also a few officers, of all ranks and regiments and of the most varied types. I began to realise how lucky I was. These people in the cellars proved to me that being frightened or not was a matter of luck, like being unmusical or short-sighted.

I knew some of them. There was Sergeant A, quite a close friend of mine back at the station. He was a good-looking chap of 28, always neatly turned out, a good pilot and top of the class in flight theory and navigation. He knew what the war was about and, like all of us, had volunteered to be a glider pilot. He was conscientious, hard-working and unsparing with himself, the kind of person whom I would have thought had all the qualifications of a good soldier. I tried to persuade him to come out of his cellar, for his own good, because he was obviously going through hell, but he simply could not make himself move and, short of using force, there was nothing I could do.

I found Staff-Sergeant G in the cellar of the gardener's house. I was even more surprised to see him so terrified and must admit I enjoyed it just for a moment. Staff-Sergeant G was the tough guy of our flight ... always getting into scraps with the chaps of other units (usually below his own rank) and called me 'la-di-da' and 'Miss

Hagen' because I wore pyjamas and did not swear. He used to brag about what he would do once he met the Germans. He would take the first German child by the legs and tear it in two … as the only good German was a dead German. There was no sense in reminding him of this because, now that he was so consumed by fear, he was only pathetic.

Seeing so many of our tough guys, including the Sergeant-Major, in such a terrified state, I realised just why these people in general used such tough language. They were frightened and wanted to give themselves courage and self-confidence. They wanted to appear fierce and fearless and thought that tough and foul language would do the trick. I noticed that those who really stood up to it cursed less the deeper they got into the fighting … they had proved themselves and did not need encouragement. To hear 'I wonder what the Second Army will come and get us out of this mess' simply stated, without a four-letter word used at least four times, gave me the same surprise as if they had suddenly expressed themselves in Ancient Greek.

Most of the officers and departments were distributed in slit-trenches. There was the Signals HQ trench, the RE's HQ, the RASC people and all the parts of the services which are represented in an airborne army. They all had to have their little offices round the Division HQ and were all working and waiting under this hellish strain. Waiting and waiting for the Second Army. The Second Army was always at the back of our minds. The thought of it made us stand up to anything; not only because we all felt we must hold on and prepare the way for it. That was our job. Everybody was always asking about it, and it was very praiseworthy the way the higher officers patiently answered this eternal question. They just said that, as far as they knew, the Second Army had encountered difficulties behind the lines but they were hoping for its early arrival. We all believed so strongly in it, and as time went on, its strength and power became almost legendary. We liked to imagine the moment when we had armour and could stand up and fight like men.

We found the Brigadier walking about regardless of the mortars. He might not even have been conscious of them any more. His job entailed visiting all day, and he couldn't possibly have done this efficiently trying to dodge the slow rain of missiles. Besides the mortars, even inside the perimeter and the Div. HQ, sniping was incessant. I must say that the professional German sniper, in his specially spotted cloak, was the most efficient and effective weapon. He could easily have broken the morale of any troops who were not in such a victorious mood as we still were. This may sound contradictory, since we had fought a defensive battle from the moment we arrived, but we knew that we were only a small group in a vast advancing army, and we felt completely superior to the German troops.

The Brigadier greeted us and, after Captain Z had told him that I had been on the patrol, laid out his map and asked me to show him exactly where it was I had found the German hideout. He also told me to draw in the movements of the armour I had observed. I was surprised to find that I felt no embarrassment talking to the Officer Commanding the whole Division. I felt as much in common with him as anyone in this battle. I proceeded to illustrate our movements on the map, using my grubby finger. It seems that I did the one thing possible to make him lose his temper. 'For crying out loud, take your filthy hand away! You're covering the whole bloody map … Why don't you get yourself a stick and point it out properly?' And he added, 'They all use their hands; I've had to tell them a hundred times.' 'Yes Sir,' and my interview continued normally.

The Brigadier told me he thought it was very interesting, but he must have known better than I did that there was nothing he could do about it. He enquired very precisely the position of the German troops round our street, and said he might be able to get the Second Army artillery from across the river to give us support and ease the situation. He even went so far as to ask me where I thought the barrage would be most effective – in the wood opposite or on the strong-point, right in front. I suggested behind the wood, as the strong-point was really very near our own lines and nothing of importance seemed to be behind it. The main German movement seemed to come from well behind the wood, towards the strong-point. This was farther away from our position, and so gave more margin for the artillery.

Later that night we really did get artillery support from across the river, but of course we couldn't tell how effective it was. We did see fires glowing in that direction, and the explosions sounded strong and very sweet to us. There was beginning to be spasmodic artillery fire from over the river, and the Brigadier told us that an artillery officer from the Second Army had arrived at Division HQ and was directing it.

Our own Colonel [Murray] now joined the group. He was a tall, striking-looking man, and the thing that everyone noticed about him was his impeccable appearance and perfectly creased trousers. He didn't even wear gaiters. He was the only man who never looked any different from the way he appeared on the parade-ground, back at the RAF station. No one has yet found out his recipe for keeping the crease in his trousers. But I found him rather pompous and conceited to talk to, and his get-up, under the circumstances, rather childish. It was he who subsequently organised our whole retreat after the Brigadier was wounded. [Brigadier (now General Sir John) Hackett later made a remarkable escape back over the Rhine, many weeks after the battle, with the help of the Dutch resistance.]

These gentlemen were now busy discussing their personal problems of higher strategy, so I retired, after asking Captain Z for permission to stay behind to see the Dutch Intelligence Officer about the information I had on the subject of Dutch Nazis. Apparently his office was in a trench some distance away. I asked my way from department to department, in other words from trench to trench, and was finally directed to the prisoner of war compound. This had been the tennis court when Division HQ had been a luxury hotel. Now the tennis was surrounded by a symmetrical zig-zag trench in which were over 200 prisoners of war. Just outside this trench were separate small dug-outs where the German officers were kept. There was one completely isolated dug-out from which projected the steel-helmeted head and broad shoulders of a very impressive figure. He remained quite motionless, like a statue, and seemed oblivious of the mortar shells. He was obviously of very high rank indeed.

I found the Prisoner of War Captain and Lieutenant in their trench and was invited to come in and join them in a cup of water. Water was very short in the Div. HQ, but the way in which it was offered made refusal impossible, and I was extremely thirsty. I was allowed to ask as many questions as I liked about the prisoners and was made to feel thoroughly at home. My own theory about their quality, and the experience I had had translating for interrogations at the beginning of the action, was confirmed by what I now heard. Except for about 100 genuine SS troops, there was nothing left of the old arrogance and cockiness. A little later I had a grand opportunity to see this again. The prisoners were shouting and calling for food. Then one of the German officers got up out of his trench. He was quite furious and shouted at them to stop that noise. The British troops, he said sarcastically, had had no food for days and were fighting and disciplined. It was a pity that the Germans had not half the courage and discipline of the British, then they wouldn't have been where they were now. Then our Prisoner of War Officer walked on to the tennis court with his hands in his pockets and stood in the middle with the most disgusted look on his face and called for the parties who had cooked yesterday's dinner.

Our two POW officers couldn't help me in my search for the Dutch Intelligence Officer [Lieutenant-Commander Arnoldus Wolters, the Liaison Officer], but they did tell me that he was in naval uniform and usually to be found in the Division HQ building, and this was a step forward. I eventually found him and gave him the information I had discovered, but he told me it was quite impossible to take all the doubtful characters and small Dutch Nazis prisoner as we hadn't the food to feed them or the time to sort them out.

He also said that all the really big wigs had gone with the Germans when the first landing occurred on Sunday. He knew of the bother we were having from civilian Dutch snipers, but explained that unless they could actually be caught red-handed, there was nothing to be done about them. On the whole I agreed with him that the population was friendly towards us. I questioned many people, and tried to find out, both in Arnhem and back at Nijmegen, if there had been any organised Dutch resistance groups operating during the German occupation. But as far as we were concerned, there was no sign of them at all – there was definitely nothing here on the lines of the invaluable and splendidly organised French Maquis. [In fact, one of the many tragedies of Arnhem was the British failure to use the Dutch Underground, which was both willing and able.]

There was one large house just outside our perimeter in which there were supposed to be 20 Dutch Nazis. The Naval Intelligence Officer said it might be a good idea for me to collect some men and go and make sure about it. A parachute officer gave me five men, and with them I crossed the main road outside the perimeter. We tried doors, shutters and anything that might give us an entry, but the house seemed to be empty. Then we shot out the lock. It was a lovely old country house, beautifully kept and furnished.

We began our systematic search in the cellars. Here we found the female members of the family huddled together in the dark. They were so terrified of us that there was no doubt about their connection with the Germans. Only when we reached the attic did we find anything that might corroborate our information. A German wireless transmitter with an aerial, still connected to batteries, was there, but there was no sign of any men in the house. We left, taking the wireless with us, after we had destroyed the batteries and aerial. The women in the cellar might easily have been sending information to the Germans, but, as the Dutch officer had said, we would have had to catch them red-handed as in the case of the snipers.

It was high time to get back, as it was lunchtime, and there was no such thing as lunch at Div. HQ. I was only just in time when I arrived back. People from the other houses were looking for me, as some civilians had come and they needed an interpreter.

I went to the top house, where they told me that there was a Dutch woman badly injured in one of the unoccupied houses. There seemed to be no sign of life there. I found the cellar door, knocked, and someone opened it. There was one candle shedding a very faint light, and at first I could make out nothing, but as my eyes got accustomed to the gloom I saw that there were eight people in the cellar. There was a jar of water, some odd chairs, a small food supply and some cushions and blankets on the floor. A very pale young woman lay on an improvised bed, and I knew that this must be the injured one. The men were surprisingly neat, in good suits; they were very quiet and courteous and there was no excitement or fuss when they explained what had happened. They pulled back the blankets from the woman's feet and showed me a mess of blood and bandages. She had been shot three days ago, but they had not been able to come out to get help because of the continuous firing. I promised to go over to the hospital and see the MO about her.

I left my Sten-gun at the lower house and made a dash across the road to one of our hospital buildings. The entire floor space was covered with casualties. They were all fully dressed and covered with army blankets. I found an officer in the passage, his arm in a sling and his head bandaged, carrying water to the rooms, and asked him for the MO. He told me that the only man who could help me was the RAMC corporal, who was in charge here. The officer found him for me, but the corporal said they were so short-staffed that they couldn't even let me have a medical orderly. He advised me to find the MO [Lieutenant-Colonel Graeme Warrack, the Deputy Director Medical Services], so I had to sprint across the other crossroads to a different building.

I found the MO in charge, giving orders about fresh water and taking stock of the jeeps still in working order. He was a big cheerful man and said to me, 'You're watching medical history being made, my boy.' He explained that it was quite impossible for him, single-handed as he was, to operate on any of the casualties; all he could do for most of his patients was to smother them with penicillin powder and leave it at that. He also informed me that I was in German territory, as the hospitals were now outside our perimeter. The enemy had taken them two days ago, and he himself, with all its occupants, were prisoners on parole. He pointed out two German soldiers who were the guards of the three buildings; at the moment they were too busy helping with the wounded to do any guarding. Apparently the German MO had arrived and suggested to him that he might like our worst casualties moved behind the German lines. But when the MO told him there were 700 of them he put his hands over his eyes and said, 'Oh mein Gott! That is impossible.' The Germans had very heavy casualties of their own, and, although they had a rear and we had not, they could never have dealt with ours as well.

It was sheer hell for the wounded; they were right in the front line. The German mortar barrage was hitting our perimeter just across the road, 24 hours on end. The streets were always swept by our own and German fire, and, until they were knocked out, our 6-pounders fired along this road at approaching German armour. Those men must have felt so terribly helpless lying there, packed like sardines, on every available inch of floor space. The vibration of each explosion made them catch their breath and groan with pain, yet when I went into one of the rooms they all asked me how we were doing and if there was any news of the Second Army.

Obviously the MO couldn't come himself, but he chose an experienced medical orderly to go with me. I showed him down the dark stairs, and he went to work immediately. The first thing he did, after seeing the injury, was to give the woman a morphia injection. Then he began the tedious and revolting process of removing the bandages. The blood had seeped through them and dried; now the dressing was a solid crust all mixed up with what was left of her toes. It took the orderly over an hour. Then he covered her mutilated feet with penicillin powder and left a bottle of this, fresh dressings and morphia with the people, in case he could not get back the next day. During the long and ghastly procedure the inhabitants of the cellar remained calm and quiet. The immediate effect of the morphia put the woman out of pain for the first time for three days. They were all touchingly grateful, though they couldn't say very much. I was glad to be able to tell them that we were only too pleased to do what we could for them, and reminded them that the Dutch were doing wonderful work, helping at the hospital.

I arrived back in our street just in time for the afternoon self-propelled gun attack. Again Lieutenant X and I were able to stop this monster from passing our Piat position. Our attic was quite a cosy little nest, although not as luxurious as the Officers' Room. I suppose it had been a maid's bedroom before it became a gun position. She would have been surprised and shocked to see the use we made of her feather bed. On it was mounted the leg of the Piat and every bomb we fired caused a snow-storm of feathers. I found that these feathers made excellent ear plugs, for my ears were becoming more and more sensitive to the noise of explosions. I appeared at my interview with the Brigadier with my ears full of feathers, and only realised later why he and the Colonel had looked at me so strangely. The old porcelain washstand in the attic was useful too, as the basin housed our loose rounds of ammunition and the flat marble top was ideal for laying out and cleaning our Bren. The nicest thing we found up there was a little hoard of food that the maid must have stored away for private snacks. This was really an ideal position from every point of view and we got more and more attached to it.

That afternoon another fleet of supply planes came over to drop urgently needed ammo and food. The cold-blooded pluck and heroism of the pilots was quite incredible. They came in, in their lumbering four-engined machines, at 1500 feet, searching for our position. The ack-ack was such as I have only heard during the worst raids on London, but concentrated on one small area. The German gunners were firing at point-blank range and the supply planes were more or less sitting targets. The rattle of machine-guns from the scores of planes, the heavy ack-ack batteries all round us, the sky filled with flashes and puffs of exploding shells, burning planes diving towards the ground, and hundreds and hundreds of red, white, yellow and blue supply parachutes dropping all in this very small area, looked more like an overcrowded and crazy illustration to a child's book. This was war on such a concentrated scale that it made you feel terribly small, frightened and insignificant: something like an ant menaced by a steam roller. All activity on the ground seemed to be suspended and forgotten on both sides. One could do nothing but stare awe-inspired at the inferno above.

How those pilots could have gone into it with their eyes open is beyond my imagination. Later on, when I got back to the 'drome, I heard something of what they had felt. And I was told of their tremendous losses.

When we saw the supply planes coming in over our position, we knew nothing of the hell they had been through already; many of them had failed to get this far. They had first had to deal with great packs of Focke-Wulfs, and in one of the trips they crossed into Holland without any fighter support as the weather did not permit it. When they met the Focke-Wulfs they had very little chance to defend themselves. The Americans were included in our boundless admiration, for they came along in their unarmed, slow, twin-engined Dakotas as regularly as clockwork. The greatest tragedy of all, I think, is that hardly any of these supplies reached us. It makes the heroism of the crews of the planes even more incredible when one realises that they must have known that there was very little chance of their sacrifice being of any use to us.

After the planes left, our usual activities of sniping and covering our approaches continued. We noticed that just across the plantation things were suspiciously quiet. A small patrol was sent over and reported that our troops had withdrawn from these houses. This was highly disturbing as it meant that our street could be surrounded on three sides. The fourth side, nearest to Div. HQ, was already under German fire, though not directly threatened. Captain Z sat up in bed and said, 'Bad show, bad show, very dangerous. Wonder what the buggers thought they were up to … Must see the Colonel about it.' We could easily have moved in now that the row of houses were empty. It was pretty obvious that Jerry would do so if we didn't, as soon as he got up enough courage. Unfortunately for us, nothing was ever done about it; I suppose the reason was that the men needed from Division HQ couldn't be spared. In any case the result was bound to be uncomfortable.

As the afternoon went on, Fearless Frank, one of our glider pilot officers, who had been decorated and earned this name in Sicily, collected some men to go on a patrol. He was a smallish, funny-looking chap, with a terrific guardee moustache that looked absurdly out of place. He had a delicate manner and a gentle voice, which he tried unsuccessfully to turn into a soldierly bark, by emitting his words in clipped splutters, and using a great deal of emphasis and jerky movements of his body.

There were ten of us on this patrol; we were supposed to attack a German-occupied house whose Spandau machine-gun was covering the main road running between the two hospitals. Fearless Frank, who was full of initiative and imagination, had quite rightly decided that the only way to deal with this position was to surprise it from the rear – a direction which Jerry would image was safely held by his own people. We couldn't really hope to overcome the position, as one side of the house was next to the hospital, the front faced the main road and the other side and the back were in the German lines. But we felt we could give them a jolly good fright, and make it quite uncomfortable for them.

We crossed the small road into a house next to the hospital building, and, from its back garden, into the wood that ran parallel to our street. It was getting dark and we managed to advance without being detected. Whilst advancing we made sure that we had a good line of withdrawal. We cut wire fences and marked trees to direct ourselves. When we got into the back garden of the house we were attacking we could hear the Spandau firing down the road from the front. We knew that our attack must be very short and concentrated – for if they had time to turn the machine-gun against us there would be little chance of our getting away. We put our Brens into position about 20 yards from the back of the house, then simultaneously we opened up with everything we had while we lobbed hand grenades into the windows.

We must have given them quite a fright, for the Spandau stopped and our fire was not returned. The house was completely quiet. It was sickening that this was all we could do; to try and storm the position would have been suicide, and anyway we couldn't have held it. There were only ten of us, with no reinforcements, and Jerryland all round us. We got back without having achieved anything definite, feeling rather vague about what we had done. It wasn't really satisfying.

There were now definite signs that the Germans were moving into the houses across the plantations, just as we had feared. We started to prepare for this new threat. New firing positions had to be fixed up in the back room, the trenches altered so that we could fire in both direction, and bricks taken out of a windowless outhouse in our garden, which made an ideal sniping position. This new situation was very annoying; it meant that we would have to man still more positions and get still less sleep, apart from the very uncomfortable feeling of being attacked from the rear. We heard Jerry moving about and shouting, but only an odd burst of fire came from this direction during the night. He was firing at us more than ever from the wood, and the large house which stood back in the trees was beginning to catch fire. He must have set it alight purposely, as we had noticed him using incendiary bullets and phosphorous grenades that afternoon. The flames got higher and higher, and we hoped that this would set

the whole wood alight and drive Jerry further back from our positions. Unfortunately this never happened and the ruins of the house
gave him an ideal advanced sniping position which proved a con-
tinual bother to us.

After dinner I was called into the Officers' Room and told that
several little jobs had to be done during the night and would I like
to be in on them again. A container had been dropped during the
afternoon just on the fringe of the wood opposite our houses. We
wanted to get it as soon as the flames in the burning house had died
down a little. Also, we were nearly out of small-arms ammunition and
Piat bombs, and everybody was crying out for cigarettes. We were to
try to scrounge whatever we could from Div. HQ. This time we were
going to make quite sure that the Poles would let us past their lines
and Lieutenant S took me to see the Polish officer in charge of the
house next door. We got over to their positions about 25 yards away
and managed to get into their house by making a dash for it. The
Polish officer was most friendly and helpful, and told us that he was
going to tell all his men that our patrol was going to pass later on that
night. But we wouldn't take any risks this time and we weren't satisfied until he promised us a guide to take us through. When we got
back, the fire had died down considerably, and Graham and myself
thought it was time to go and recover the container. We could not
very well ask anyone to give us covering fire as the road and the position of the container were too exposed and the chances of hitting us
or attracting the attention of the enemy were too great. We dashed
over and started dragging the container across the road. It was almost
impossible to move and, as the burning house was still lighting up this
part of the street, everybody must have been able to see us. We had to
get across now or never. Thank God the house opposite us was very
alert and two pilots came dashing out. The four of us managed to pull
the container into the garden. Now that there wasn't such a desperate
hurry, we thought it incredible that we had managed to move it at all,
because when we tried to drag it further behind the house we could

not move it an inch. We opened the container excitedly and found eight wooden boxes; when we broke them open, two large shiny 17-pounder shells were disclosed. One can imagine how pleased we were with our work! If ever there were any 17-pounder guns in our sector they must have been knocked out right in the beginning. We now had the nice job of disposing of them as we could not risk them being blown up by German mortars or shells.

We had a short rest in the Officers' Room and by twelve midnight were on our way to the Div. HQ. The patrol consisted of Lieutenant X, Graham, the Polish guide and myself. We crawled along the plantation, very careful not to attract the attention of the new German position, and all went well for a bit. Suddenly, out of the dark, a voice said something quite unintelligible, sharp and short. It was obviously a Pole challenging us and we looked towards our Polish guide, but he never made a sound. For a moment we thought we had lost him, but I could still feel him next to me lying flat on the ground, his gun pointing towards the voice in the dark; he was trembling. I hissed to him, 'Talk in Polish'. No result whatsoever. We had now taken up the same position behind cover, ready to fire the moment we were attacked. Lieutenant X came crawling back very carefully and poked the Pole in the ribs and whispered, 'Why don't you challenge him in Polish, bloody fool?' But it was not good at all; he remained completely paralysed with fright. The voice in the dark now whispered very fiercely, and it sounded to us like an ultimatum. I started muttering 'British, British' and the password of the day, but the voice seemed to be quite unaware of what I was talking about. We began to move forward now, but the dangerous hissing sound out of the dark made us stop dead. We were in a great state of agitation and I felt mad at our guide. This was a complete deadlock, and the prospect of spending the night there didn't seem very attractive to any of us. We had to try again. Our guide was apparently deaf and dumb, and we pushed him towards the Polish voice, thinking that they might recognise each other when they were near enough. This was a great success. They more or less fell into each other's arms, gibbering like two school-girls, and we went into the nearest house, leaving the happy couple behind. We asked for the officer, and after long discussions in sign language, they managed to produce him. Luckily the Polish officer spoke English and realised the danger we were in. He produced one of his men, whom he said could talk English, and we continued our journey. We managed to get past the other Polish-occupied houses with the aid of our new guide, nor was the crossing of the main road to the HQ very hard.

We groped our way to the cellar of the large hotel building. Down there was housed the nerve centre of the Division. Lieutenant X went into the Intelligence Office to report on our position and find out about orders, etc. We waited in the dark gangway. There was an amazing coming and going in the total darkness, everybody tip-toeing and feeling their way quietly, as the floor of the passage was lined on both sides with stretchers on which lay recent casualties. There was a first-aid room with a doctor on one side of this passage, and this was so overcrowded during the night that the wounded could not all be harboured in there. A voice called out 'Anybody know any German here?' I felt my way towards the first-aid room and was asked to interpret for the MO who was attending to a German prisoner. This was a boy of about eighteen or nineteen; his hand and wrist were badly shot up; he looked desperately pale and frightened. He wanted to say something and no one in the room could make out what it was. He said in a small and frightened voice, 'What are they going to do with me now? I was made to fight. It's not my fault.' The doctor made me translate that he shouldn't worry and that he was going to be treated exactly the same as any of our wounded and sent to hospital at the earliest opportunity. His sigh of relief and happy smile made him look quite different. He asked me if we could find his parents when we went into Germany as they had no idea where he was and what had happened to him. I had to take his name and address down, and he was not satisfied until I had done this and given it to the doctor.

Every single German I talked to or watched being interrogated kept on saying that he was made to be a soldier and forced to fight us. It was rather monotonous. The idea of our chaps behaving similarly when taken prisoner by the Germans seemed very funny to me – it was so entirely out of the question. The difference between us and them was that we knew we were right and they knew they were doing wrong and therefore had a guilty conscience. I thought it strange that our German propaganda could not make more use of this tremendous advantage. The thing that most likely stopped them from following this up must have been the policy of unconditional surrender. I wondered if this policy was really worth it.

Lieutenant X came out and said that we could look for the ammo ourselves in the ammunition compound. He had been unsuccessful in getting us any cigarettes, and there was no news of the Second Army, but it still might arrive at any time. It was a painful job looking for the compound. We stumbled into slit-trenches and were pushed out as quickly as we fell in by sleep-drunk soldiers. We were forced to fall flat on our faces time and time again when the shriek of mortars sounded dangerously near. We got there eventually, but what a pathetic ammunition store for a whole division! We could easily have shifted the whole lot into our attic and still had enough space to fire our Piat. Even what there was was not much use, as most of it was 3-inch mortar shells and other kinds of ammo for which there were no weapons.

We did get some ordinary rounds for the Brens and rifles, however, but no Sten ammunition and no 2-inch mortar shells. We couldn't find any Piat bombs either, but Graham remembered having seen some in one of the houses opposite the main road. We made our way back there. He must have had an amazing sense of direction for we found them in complete darkness, hidden under some bushes. Our little expedition had turned out to be quite a successful.

Sunday

At stand-to next morning I was asked about the success of our patrol to Division HQ. What was meant by this was had we brought back any cigarettes? I was considered a complete failure and, to minimise my humiliation, I suggested that they should try smoking the long leaves which hung from the roof of the outdoor building at the back of our house. These were obviously tobacco leaves. Someone cried out, 'Dutch tobacco! Famous the whole world over!' I thought of the terrible disappointment they would feel after they'd smoked the stuff. Their resentment would come back to roost on me. An argument arose about tobacco in general. Someone said that the really good Dutch tobacco came from the colonies, another said that this grown in Holland was the real stuff. Some claimed they had smoked it already. I left them squabbling, knowing that they would find out only too soon. They started to dry the leaves over an open fire and soon everyone was rolling the result in the palms of their hands and stuffing their pipes. The kitchen had to be evacuated almost at once, but some enthusiasts, who were suffering particularly, kept on smoking this filthy concoction till our first cigarette issue in Nijmegen.

The small-arms fire and sniping this morning was worse than anything we had had before. It was doubly effective now. It came from the row of houses across the plantation, as well as from the wood. Our special enemy was the burnt-out house directly opposite us. This was a sniper's paradise and Jerry was using some kind of apparatus to throw hand grenades from behind the house against our façade and barricaded windows. These continuous explosions right under our noses were really very uncomfortable. Our barricades of the windows and doors had to be redone every time the blast of a grenade threw them back into the room. There is nothing more irritating than a grenade bounding into a furnished room and rolling perhaps under the bed, where it can't be fished out and thrown back before it explodes.

The solution to our troubles would have been simply to knock the building flat with mortars or our Piat gun, but we had no mortar bombs at all, and the Piat bombs we had collected could not be spared for a job of this sort.

I changed my Bren-gun position from the attic into the front room of the second floor. I started to give them bursts any time I could detect the slightest movement. Smithy was beside me, sniping with his rifle through a hole in the wall near the window. The crackling of small arms fire was like a bonfire. The Germans had probably detected our firing positions. We could hear the thud of the bullets on the outside wall and the shape of each window was outlined and filled in by a pattern of bullet holes on the wall behind us. Each time they hit the edge of the windows a spray of chips, splinters and plaster made us jump aside. They seemed to be giving Smithy and me all their attention.

Suddenly Smithy shouted, 'I've been hit.' His whole wrist and hand were soaked in blood. He lay on the floor whilst I tried to tie a bit of rag round the wound to stop the bleeding. Then we both crawled across the room to the door and I shouted for someone to help him down the stairs into the Officers' Room. I had to stay up there as the Bren was too valuable for our defence to be left inactive.

I poked my barrel through the hole that Smithy had left and started firing at some movement I detected. Then a sudden terrific bang … I thought this was my turn. My hand was covered with blood and I withdrew the gun quickly. I wiped the blood away, expecting to find a serious injury as I could feel no pain at all, and discovered that a splinter had just penetrated a vein and this was causing the bleeding. And then I noticed my Bren barrel and realised how incredibly lucky I had been. A bullet had entered the flash-eliminator that widens the barrel at the end, split it open and by some miracle ricocheted off again, instead of going into me. The good old gun still worked, but I had to exchange barrels at the earliest opportunity. Anyhow, after a few minutes the signal for my morning session in the attic was heard from the top of the street, and, calling to Lieutenant X, I fetched the Piat and went up the stairs, quite confident, and taking my time. By now we knew the slow and careful approach of our old friend, the German self-propelled gun.

This morning, though, they had a surprise for us. They manoeuvred two of them into position, one on each side of the road. The terrific small-arms attack seemed to show that they were working up for real business. We were glad we had fetched those 20 bombs last night, as with two SPs firing shells incessantly as they advanced, we had to lay a screen across the road. This was our only hope of stopping them. They stopped dead for a while, just out of range, and then retired slowly. The small-arms activity died down to normal and we knew we had repelled them again, anyhow for the moment.

It suddenly became a pleasant Sunday morning. Our regular Arnhem hotpot was simmering, the Red Cross appeared on the streets, and everyone came down for a breather to see how the food was getting on and how the others were. Eating our food, the reaction from the heavy attack made us quite gay and we compared our near misses. Everybody boasted and produced proof. I thought I had a pretty good story to tell, but when I saw some of the others I knew that this morning's battle honours were not mine. Like all of us, Tony wore a sort of false bosom under his battle-smock. This consisted of his personal belongings and ammunition. A bullet has passed through this bosom, into his water bottle, smashed up the pin of a hand grenade in his top pocket and passed out again. His first reaction had been fear that he was mortally wounded, for water from his bottle was trickling down his body and he naturally thought this must be blood. After examining himself, he removed all his belongings and got an even worse fright when he pulled out a live grenade minus the pin. He had thrown it away before he realised what he was doing, and the fright (though of course he said it was the explosion) knocked him for six. Anybody who survived an experience like that deserved to get out alive, and Tony did.

The next of this morning's heroes was Fitz. His private bullet, which he now thinks of with great affection, entered his false bosom and ripped his smock and the tunic beneath it three-quarters of the way across his chest, just above his heart. There were many minor escapees like myself with my Bren-gun. I fetched this down proudly and passed it round the kitchen. Then Vic discovered that my left epaulette had been split across by a bullet. I felt I could not join the other two on equal terms. As a matter of fact, none of us could hold a candle to our private miracle man. This glider pilot was the pride of our street, because by all the laws of nature he ought to have been dead, and instead he was doing kitchen fatigues quite happily.

A bullet had entered his right temple and exited through his left, leaving behind it a couple of neat little holes. He wasn't even knocked out of the fight by this and had to be ordered sternly not to take part in combatant duties. Not only did he remain working in the kitchen all of the time we were in our house, but he was able to retreat with us across the Rhine. The last we saw of him he was sitting perkily in the back of an ambulance in Belgium, making rude signs at us as he passed. An MO whom we told about it later, said that this was possible, as the front part of the brain governs the emotions, and an injury to it does not necessarily cause any organic change. He explained that the work done by the damaged part of the brain would be taken on temporarily by another part. And he added that quite often people injured in this way become very cheerful to start with and feel stimulated. This, of course, does not last for long, but would account for the way our miracle man behaved.

Sunday afternoon was fairly quiet, but towards dusk the firing increased sharply. Before we knew what was happening it developed into the first direct assault on our position. Somehow Jerry had crossed the road from the wood into the next house. I hadn't seen it happen, so they might have come from the plantation in our rear. The first thing I saw were the tops of German helmets moving along the space between the two houses, which only gave them very slight cover. I had to get a firing line from my attic to them, which meant removing several tiles, and by the time I got into position they were firing at us with an automatic gun. I could take my time aiming and getting ready as it was very unlikely that they would detect me. After my first burst the German who was firing disappeared and his gun toppled over on to the veranda. Either myself, or someone else firing in the same direction, had hit one or more of them. I started looking round for new victims. It was getting dark now and difficult to make out what was going on. Right underneath me next door, only about 3 yards away, a window was pushed open and I saw people moving inside the room. So the Germans were here! This room had always been empty and lately the whole house had been evacuated to strengthen the top corner position. They were trying to get out of the window into our house and I could not fire at them from where I was as they were too close underneath me. I ran from my attic to a side window on the second floor to lob a hand grenade into the room. I heard it break some glass and a few seconds later it exploded. When my eyes got used to the darkness again, I could still see movement in the room after it had exploded. I couldn't make out why I had not killed everyone in there and threw, one after another, my remaining store of grenades. And still there was movement in the room. I was just going to run down and fetch some more hand grenades to deal with this apparent wave of Germans when a controlled and quiet voice called up to me, 'What do you think you are doing?' Trying to kill us all?' My heart stood still for a moment. Then I realised what I had been doing. I was certain I had killed and injured many of them; it was the worst moment of the whole seven days, and I wished I was dead myself. I jumped down the stairs out of the house and across to the other one through the window and into the room. Everything looked quite normal there, except for the miracle man lying on the bed with a bandage round his head and the Lieutenant and three others sitting on the floor. I told them that it was I who had thrown the grenades, and where were the casualties? He said, 'Oh, it was you, was it? Thank God you didn't know your job. At such short distance you should have waited four seconds until you threw; that gives another three seconds until the grenade explodes. As it was, we lobbed them out of the window as fast as you threw them. They all exploded just outside, and you're a fool not to have noticed it.' I was never more grateful for being a fool!

The others had been fighting hard all round the house, as the enemy had tried to get at us from every side. It began to get quieter and it seemed as if they had had enough. Next morning we found several bodies, amongst them my Jerry machine-gunner.

I was called to the Officers' Room and Captain Z told me to wake him at 1 a.m. as he had to report to the Brigadier at 2 a.m. I was to go with him to Div. HQ, so I made my bed, and Lieutenant X, who was duty officer for that period, promised to wake me in time. It was hell to get up at this hour of the morning for I had only had two hours' sleep. The light was dim and it was peaceful and warm. Captain Z's full rosy cheeks, and the regular vibrations of the ends of his moustache, made a picture of peace and content. I could hardly bring myself to wake him. I shook him gently, but soon realised that sterner measures would have to be used. I pulled the sheets and eiderdown off him, shook him roughly and shouted at him, 'Captain Z, you have to get up to go to the Div. HQ.' 'Who's giving orders here?' he replied. 'The Brigadier, sir, and it's nearly half-past one.'

We arrived in the cellar at Div. HQ; the little room of the Intelligence people was very crowded and no one took any notice of us. Everyone was half asleep and could hardly keep his eyes open. I reported the glider pilot section under Captain Z present and pointed out on the map our position, and that of the enemy. There were no orders for the next day, except to carry on as usual, and a bit of encouragement by telling us that we had been doing well. We went on another scrounge and returned with a few Piat bombs and several hundred rounds of rifle ammo.

Monday

It was nearly dawn on Monday morning by the time we got back, so we helped the Duty Officer and the Sergeant-Major to wake everybody and get ready for the stand-to. The firing slowly increased from all sides, but we did not have to cope with any strong attacks. I think we must have inflicted fairly heavy casualties yesterday evening and so discouraged Jerry from another assault. We were all desperately tired by now and everyone seemed to be sleep-walking and dozing off every now and then at their firing positions. I felt like a very slow and heavy machine, doing everything automatically, but at half speed. The whole morning was quieter than it had ever been before and the lack of action made us feel our weariness. The self-propelled guns did not even appear during the morning. There seemed to be a complete deadlock at our sector. Probably Jerry was preparing a big attack. We were hoping for the Second Army. This morning gave us a chance to think and we realised that we could not hold on for ever without being reinforced. Lunch cheered us up again, and I quite enjoyed hearing an increase in the German small-arms fire, as it meant we had to fire back, and that was the only way to keep awake.

Captain Z and another captain came back from Division HQ and the officers from the other houses came filing through our kitchen into the Officers' Room. Something was up. Rumours began to circulate at once. The Second Army was on its way; we were going to withdraw; we were going to attack; our street was going to be withdrawn into the perimeter; and so on and so on. The officers' huddle went on for two hours and the rumours went on circulating.

At last we were told to go and see the Captain in groups of four for the night's orders. I went in. A large map was spread on the table. In a confident voice, Captain Z began the briefing. We were going to retreat across the Rhine and join the Second Army. It was going to be an orderly and organised withdrawal. All sections were to leave their sectors at a specified time with all their arms and ammunition. Our street was going to leave at ten-fifteen. The men from the top corner house would move in to the next house; from there they would all move into the next, and so on until the entire glider pilot section were all in the house nearest the perimeter. From there he pointed out the route that we were going to take to the river. It lay mostly through woods and along little paths, and the more we tried to memorise it the harder we knew it was going to be. All except Captain Z. He fairly radiated optimism.

When I came out of the Officers' Room into the kitchen, quite a few of the chaps were stuffing themselves with food, trying to lay up a store of energy for whatever might be coming. It seemed criminal to be leaving any food behind and no one had any idea when his next meal was going to be. I thought it very wise and joined the party. Lieutenant X and two other men worked their way through the shadowy kitchen carrying a stretcher. Bill had been killed the night before and had to be buried. We stood up, and there was a minute's silence as they passed out through the back door, then we went on with our supper.

I got my gun ready and clean, collected odd Sten-gun rounds from all the rooms in the house, and filled the empty mags. I was hoping for two hours' rest, but firing had increased so much that we had to go out and man all the positions. We didn't want to run any risks at this particular moment and we wanted to give an impression of complete normality. We had been specially warned at the briefing not even to discuss the coming withdrawal among ourselves, for fear of listening Germans or civilians. Any leakage would have resulted in a bloody slaughter. All our boots were to be covered in sacking and those who got hold of civilian shoes were to hang their boots round their necks. We were supposed to blacken our faces, but this was hardly necessary, with a week's growth of beard and no washing. The order for the whole Division was to withdraw in single file, fully armed, and without noise.

It may have been nerves or over-anxiety to appear normal, but all along our street our positions started blazing against the Jerry lines.

I was pleased to notice that his reply was not over-energetic. I stood with Vic and Cooper in the trench, peering out into the darkness and burying 3-inch mortar shells which we had never been able to use during the whole action. I was leaving the trench to try and find a spade when a burst of fire came straight at us from the next house. Someone said, 'They've hit me,' and we found Cooper leaning against the wall holding his right arm. We took him up to the kitchen and then dashed back to the trench. We knew it must have been someone from the next house and went down the trench towards it. There was no one on guard there and we entered the side door. The entrance was crowded with chattering Polish soldiers. Before I could find their officer, one of them had elbowed his way through and asked me how many of us were killed or injured. I told him that we had been very lucky and his men had only hit one of our chaps. A soldier came up to me, talking very excitedly with tears in his eyes. Someone came and translated. He wanted to know if he had killed or seriously injured anyone, and was terribly relieved when he heard that all four bullets had gone into the arm of only one man. He went on to explain that he thought the Germans had infiltrated the trench and, when there was no reply to his challenge, he fired some rounds. There was nothing one could do; but it was specially sad, as it was 9 o'clock now and it would give Cooper very little chance to recover in time for the withdrawal. Besides, orders were not to take any injured men with us; but, in actual fact, Cooper stood up to the strain of the withdrawal and I saw him safely in a hospital with the Second Army.

It was nearly zero hour. Captain Z called me to the Officers' Room and told me to stick to him all through the withdrawal. More and more men from the other houses were coming down to our position, waiting for Captain Z to lead them to safety. We moved off, Captain Z and myself leading. Behind us a silent, long file of about 50 glider pilots. We made our way steadily to Div. HQ. It was easy for us as we had been this way every night. We wound our way through the mass of slit trenches, trying to avoid any obstacle which might break the long chain. It was a black night, and the noise of the dripping from the trees covered the sound of our footsteps. We passed within 50 yards of the prisoner of war compound. Up to now we hadn't met a single soul and even when I looked over to the old tennis court I could not see any movement whatsoever. Firing ahead of us could be heard quite distinctly, mostly bursts of machine-gun and the thud of exploding mortars. We were leaving our old perimeter now and moving through a kind of no-man's-land towards the river. The Germans had not been able to occupy this part thoroughly, but machine-gun nests and strong-points were dotted about in the woods. It was about 4 miles from her to the river and the problem was to get there, avoiding these danger spots.

Captain Z still seemed pretty sure of the route he was taking, but the denser the woods and undergrowth became, the more difficult it was to follow the path. In front of us was a large meadow and we had to find a way round it; we could not risk crossing it openly. From then onwards it was more or less intuition and the colossal luck of Captain Z that brought us to our destination. He felt his way forward, muttering to me, 'We'll make it yet, don't worry, you stick to me … Do you think we are all right, old boy?' I didn't have the slightest idea whether we were all right or where we were, nor had anyone else. I felt rather like the blind leading the blind. Miraculously, we came upon a farmhouse which we recognised as having been marked on the map. We knew we had to take the lane to the left of this and we followed it. Machine-guns could be heard ahead of us and, as our column halted to climb over a fence, a breathless officer appeared out of the darkness and told us to turn round immediately as his column had run straight into a German Spandau and he thought he was the only one who had survived. His head was bleeding and he had tied a bandage round it himself. We turned round, everyone following the man in front, until the leading part of the column had overtaken the tail. The men were remarkably silent and disciplined and there was no shuffling or pushing. Captain Z asked me to go along the line and call

all the men with Sten-guns to the front. This was the most dangerous part of our journey; we might run into the enemy at any moment. On and on we walked through the dark wood, turning and winding whenever we felt we were too near the enemy. I was walking in front of Captain Z, my finger on the trigger, prepared for anything. I had lost all sense of time or distance and groped my way forward wher-ever he directed me. We emerged from the wood and in front of us stretched a wide plain. This was the approach to the river. Someone came up and led us along the fringe of the wood. We followed him until we came to a white tape which was stretched across the plain. We were to follow this until we reached the river. 'We've done it again, we've done it again!' Captain Z whispered excitedly to me as the long column followed the seemingly endless white tape across the meadows. From the wood behind us firing could be heard and we wondered if they had found us out. Mortar shells were passing over, exploding not very far in front. The crossing was not going to be easy; we knew that by now.

The tape led us to a hedge and continued alongside it, eventually passing through to the other side, on to a path running down towards the river. The mortar barrage must have shifted, or even stopped, and the relief at the thought of a safe crossing was wonderful. Captain Z said, 'Look, the poor dead cow.' Then we began to see human bodies lying all along the path. As we continued, we saw that some of them were moving and heard groans and weak cries for help. A voice in the dark was muttering and talking in delirium. This was more than I could stand and I knelt down by one of the injured men. I called for three of our chaps to help me take him down to the river. The wounded man begged us not to leave him behind and to help him across the river. We tried to lift him, but he groaned with pain and we had to lay him down again.

Then as my eyes got used to the open darkness of the meadow, searching for the origin of subdued screams, I began to distinguish the shapes of bodies dragging themselves towards the path. Feverish pleading eyes looked up towards me, arms clutched around my legs, it seemed that all the wounded were frenzied by the fear of being left behind. For the first time during the whole action I panicked. I dragged limp bodies along towards the beach. I ran around in circles searching for someone in command and pleading with uninjured men to give me a hand. I vomited and felt faint. Then someone with an authoritative voice came up from the river and ordered me to leave the wounded where they were as they could not be got over the river just now and a doctor would be left behind to look after them. Exhausted and dazed by my impotence and the ghastliness of the scene, I continued towards the river.

All along the path there were mortar pits and the bodies of dead and wounded soldiers. We reached the banks of the Rhine and joined a long queue of men waiting to be ferried across. Someone came up to us and told us to spread out as the mortaring might be resumed any minute. There were at least 100 men in front of us and no sign of a boat. There were other parties like ours all along the river, waiting. The splash of oars could be heard now and then. I suppose this was how they felt at Dunkirk. A small canvas boat was approaching at last. It took ten men across. Then we realised our desperate position. Any moment the mortaring might start again. There was no cover at all and we crouched in the deep squelchy mud. We were frozen with cold and soaked from the rain.

The mortaring started up again, not directly where we were, but near enough to be frightening. After trenches and street fighting, and even the cover of the woods, we felt helplessly exposed. The thought of those ghastly bodies and the groans of the wounded, lying in the meadows, was in everyone's mind, but no one said anything. We just crouched there shivering.

I began surveying our position in my mind. Of course this had nothing in common with Dunkirk, and those who ordered us to wait in line patiently until we were taken off by those ridiculous little canvas assault boats did not know what they were doing. The Rhine was only 250 yards wide and quite narrow at certain spots near us. Why was not the order given for those of us who could swim to dump their arms and make for the other side? Surely it would have been possible to organise a rope and stretch it across for those who were not strong swimmers? But instead we were being heroic, play-ing at Dunkirk, and a great many men who could have escaped to safety would be casualties or else be taken prisoner at dawn.

I had to get out of this. I told Captain Z that I couldn't stand this any longer and that I was going to try and swim for it. Now we had got this far I didn't intend to take any more risks than were necessary. The boat system was obviously hopelessly inadequate and, apart from relieving some of this awful congestion on the bank and leaving the boats, such as they were to the non-swimmers, I honestly thought it was the best way out. He agreed with me and shouted to the rest of our glider pilot section that we were going on to a promontory where the river narrowed a bit.

A large crowd followed us, but I doubt if any of them realised where we were going or what we intended to do. They just came after us because at least we seemed to have some kind of plan. Had they been told that the river was only 250 yards wide, though it looked rather more in the dark, many would have followed us, orders or no orders. We had to climb some large boulders on our way to the promontory. At the end, it went steeply down into the water and would have made a far better landing stage for the rescue boats than the mud flats, as at least the bank gave a little cover. From here the opposite bank didn't look too far and the prospect of doing something after the misery of queuing up on all fours in the mud made Captain Z, and me feel quite cheerful. 'We'll do it again, you and me!' he said. We proceeded to take our boots off and hung them round our necks. Captain Z gave his rifle to Lieutenant X, who unfortunately couldn't swim, and remarked that he must keep his haversack with him as the Company 'Office' etc., was in it. I kept all my arms and ammo as we couldn't be sure what would greet us on the other side.

I put my Sten-gun across my shoulders and, by the time I was ready, Captain Z was in the water and swimming away from the bank. In I went. The water was pleasantly warm, the air filling my battle smock kept me easily afloat. I felt happy and full of confidence. Captain Z was about 20 yards in front of me, but drifting fast downstream. The current was very strong and I tried hard to work against it so as to reach the other bank more or less opposite where the promontory stood. Captain Z seemed to be getting on all right and I couldn't catch him up, as my battle-smock gradually deflated and swimming became harder and harder. I began to get worried and breathe fast and I was only half-way across. Then I wasn't doing proper strokes any more and I began to panic. Like a flash it came to me that this was the one fatal thing to do and the best possible way to get drowned. How ridiculous it would seem that I, brought up as I had been by a lake, and a swimmer since I was four, should die by drowning in the calm warm waters of the Rhine after evading every kind of violent death for the last seven days.

I turned over on my back to rest and pull myself together. I realised that I had to get rid of my Sten-gun, but that would be pretty difficult as it was strapped round my back. I had to let myself sink vertically while I eased the gun up and over my head. A moment later I heard it go bubbling to the bottom. Next, I methodically rid myself of all the impediments that my battle smock contained, also my boots and steel helmet. There were Sten-gun mags, hand grenades, writing materials, my fountain pen and every conceivable thing I had managed to save. Unfortunately I couldn't discriminate in the water, and all my belongings, including my AB 64 [identity papers], went floating down the Rhine.

The difference was marvellous. I felt like I had when I'd been bathing a fortnight ago in the Thames, except that it was dark. I looked round for Captain Z, but there was no sign of him at all. I shouted and began to swim round, but there was no reply and I supposed he had already got to the far bank. I swam on alone. Fires were burning on both sides of the river and the mortaring was still going on. There was an increased rattle of machine-guns from the wood we had left only an hour ago, but I felt I was beyond this, enclosed by the still warm waters. I might never have been on the other side.

I was about 20 yards from land when I saw two figures gesticulating wildly and heard shouting: 'Hold on, mate, hold on. We'll be there in a moment. Don't panic, it's OK, you're safe now.' They were preparing to plunge into the water and pull me out when I shouted to them not to bother and that I was perfectly all right. Two pairs of hands seized me and pulled me out. Nothing would convince these enthusiastic life-savers that I didn't need artificial respiration. Maybe they'd been on a course some time and this was their unique chance to practice the real thing. They tried to turn me upside down, but only succeeded in pushing me face downwards into the mud. They wouldn't let me walk on my own, but tried to lift me. This was quite impossible on the slippery ground, and anyway I would probably have been more able to carry them as they were rather undersized.

I did all I could to persuade them to let me go on alone while they stayed behind to watch for other swimmers, especially Captain Z. I began to be very worried about him when they told me that no one had come across this way and I was the first they had 'saved'. But they insisted on coming with me.

I was shivering and slipping about on the muddy ground, but what the hell? I was here and so was the Second Army. We slid and stumbled along for about fifteen minutes until we met a medical orderly. The two cockneys instructed him to take me to the first-aid post and not to stand any nonsense if I tried to escape. They said in very important voices, 'He swum the Rhine and we fished him out.' As far as they were concerned I was still drowned.

We joined a long stream of shivering men walking to the main road. Then we turned left to an open space where some lorries were parked. These were supposed to be for the wounded, but the orderly bundled me in and, as I was terribly cold and weary and had no boots,

I didn't protest too loudly. We drove along without lights, as this side of the river was also under enemy fire. Each time the lorry bumped round the edge of a shell hole the injured groaned and swore.

We stopped in front of the tents of a first-aid post and were helped out and taken inside by medical orderlies. A queue was slowly filing past several tables on which were assembled bandages, syringes, bottles and files, etc. Medical officers and orderlies were treating the walking casualties with lightning speed and efficiency. There was nothing for me to do but join the queue, as particulars were being taken and instructions given by a clerk sitting at the last table of all. I reached the first table shivering more than ever and was passed on without comment to an orderly who painted something on my forehead and was about to give me a morphia injection when I protested energetically. He replied curtly, 'I'm treating for shock here; you'll feel fine in a minute.' He went on with the treatment until I had to resort to physical violence. This made things worse; he now thought I was a really bad shock case with a touch of neurosis thrown in. He fetched a doctor and I explained that there was absolutely nothing wrong with me, except that I was very cold and wet. With the help of another orderly I undressed and my wet uniform was thrown on a large pile of soaked and bloody garments, and that was the last I saw of it. They wrapped me in blankets, gave me a cup of very sweet tea, sat me on a chair and lit a little oil-stove underneath me. Then they put a cigarette in my mouth. I was in paradise.

Several ambulances were waiting outside; they were for the walking wounded, to take them on the next stage of their journey, en route for Nijmegen. I climbed into a very crowded one and, at the next stop, managed to join a group of soldiers who were going to Nijmegen, where everyone who had escaped was supposed to report. I was still bare-foot and draped in blankets, like a Roman emperor, but found that there was no need to be self-conscious, as I was by no means the only one improperly dressed. We piled out of the lorries and filed into a large hall. A sort of improvised banquet was awaiting us; there were candles on the tables, wine glasses full of rum, and the most delicious and enormous three-course supper, rounded off with the inevitable cup of tea. Our headquarters staff, including cooks, quartermaster's staff, etc., had been waiting here to join us in Arnhem, along with the Second Army. It was they who prepared this wonderful reception for us. As we left the hall we gave our names and numbers to our squadron clerks and were given a ticket bearing the room number and barracks where we were to sleep. It was all very touching and efficient.

I spent the next twelve hours sleeping dreamlessly in a beautifully made bed.

When I woke up it occurred to me that I couldn't walk about Nijmegen still dressed as a Roman emperor, as our barracks was right in the middle of the town. Our own quartermaster stores lorry, filled with most necessities, was waiting outside and I was able to procure enough garments to cover my nakedness. The rest I scrounged from all sorts of other stores and places.

A parade was called and many of the officers and men who had only arrived during the morning, and had had to walk all the way from the river, had to be collected from wherever they were. The roll was called by an officer in the same sort of undress as I had been when I arrived. He called each name and, if the man was not present, anyone who knew his whereabouts or fate had to speak up. We stood outside the barracks, near the air-raid shelters in which hundreds of Dutch civilians were living. There was no air raid or shelling just now, so they collected round us to see the spectacle. Every time the officer had to write down a report of a missing man, his blanket had a strong tendency to slip down, and everyone watched, fascinated. From time to time it did fall right down before anyone could warn him. The civilian women looked away modestly. He didn't seem to take any notice as his job was far too important for him to worry about a detail like that.

The lovely dining-hall where we had eaten the night before received a direct hit during the morning, so we had to queue up at the cookhouse for our plentiful lunch. By now we were getting used to civilisation again and were thinking how good it would be to sleep and live in one of these charming and spotless Dutch houses surrounding the barracks. Vic and I decided to go on patrol – we had got the habit. We didn't venture very far, but went to a house just opposite, where I asked the Mevrouw if she could lend us a needle and thread as my poor friend had torn his trousers. She was only too delighted to do the job herself and Vic sat comfortably in Mijnheer's easy chair and dressing-gown. Eventually we cadged an invitation to stay the night there and use the house as if it were our own. This was just what we wanted, and most satisfactory. We wound up our stay in Nijmegen with an Anglo-Dutch party. We ate scrounged Second Army rations and drank Dutch cognac.

Before we left, General Browning called the remnants of the Division together and made an impressive and very sensible speech. We were in no mood to hear about glory and battle honours and the thanks of the motherland. We had lost, or had to leave behind, too many of our friends. But we were interested to know if the sacrifice of this Airborne Division [1st Airborne Division] would prove to have been of any use, and why the Second Army had not been able to join up with us. General Browning told us quite straightforwardly what we wanted to know. We realised what he must have felt, waiting with the Second Army, and knowing better than we ever did just how desperate our position was.

We were glad to leave Nijmegen, as what we were all longing for was a spell of complete safety. We simply loathed the air raids and spent our time diving into shelters along with the civilians, and once we had slept off our first weariness we didn't care for sleeping on the top floors of the barracks. A London civilian would have put us to shame. The idea of being killed in an air raid, after surviving all the dangers of the past days, was more than anyone could stand.

On Thursday morning the whole Division left in one huge convoy along the main Nijmegen-Brussels road. The civilians, who had been most friendly and hospitable, came searching through the crowd of waiting soldiers to say good bye to their special friends. We departed with souvenirs and gifts. All the way to Louvain we passed one continuous stream of transport, tanks, artillery, petrol lorries, jeeps, ducks [DUKWs – amphibious vehicles] and RAF vehicles. The Second Army was every bit as strong as we had imagined it. We knew that it would be able to finish the job we had had to abandon.

In parts of the road, where the corridor was especially narrow, we were still shelled by German artillery, and British tanks were covering the crossroads. Right down to Brussels the road was lined with burnt-out Allied and German transport, armoured cars and tanks. Here and there were groups of crosses with German or British steel helmets on them. There were villages completely devastated, and scores of burnt-out tanks clustered together. These must have been the scenes of German breakthroughs into the corridor, and the eventual defeat of these columns.

Everything was prepared for us in Louvain and we lined up for our supper, tea and dinner combined as soon as we arrived in the late afternoon. There weren't any air raids, but the lovely town and library were very badly damaged. We spent the evening pub-crawling and making friends with the Belgians. We drank lots of cognac. Early next morning we visited the vegetable market. It was overflowing with fruit and the most delicious grapes. The Belgian peasants would hardly allow us to pay for any of our purchases. It was surprising how enthusiastic they still were; after all, we weren't the first Allied troops to enter the city [nearby Brussels had been liberated on 3 September].

Later in the morning we were taken to an aerodrome and embarked for England. I slept the whole way across and so can give no account of a reaction – tears in my eyes or lump in my throat – to the sight of the White Cliffs. I suppose that makes this story rather incomplete.

By the evening I was back at my own 'drome. I had been away twelve days. It seemed like one day, or a lifetime.

Our huts had been locked and left just as they were when we left them on Monday morning. We took the keys, went in and sat down on our beds. The four of us looked round the hut. There were eighteen empty beds. It was very quiet now and we remembered the noise and bustle there had always been before we went away.

Supper was waiting for us in the mess. Tonight we didn't have to queue up, we were waited on by RAF pilots and WAAF. A party of all ranks was in full swing in the NAAFI. This was for us. They had expected us much earlier and a cordon of strong men was thrown round the two remaining beer barrels; but all the same our hosts were already well away and were sending sorties of shock troops to break the cordon. An RAF pilot officer was helped on to a table to deliver a speech of welcome. It wasn't long nor was it very profound, but it was received with an ear-splitting 'Hip-Hip-Hooray'. Then we were called on to answer it.

A glider pilot was carried on to the table. He spoke rather well, more coherently than the pilot officer – this was understandable. He said how much we had appreciated the gallant efforts of the RAF to reinforce us; this had struck him as the most heroic feat of the whole action. He thanked the whole ground staff for the magnificent work they had done, getting the gliders and tugs ready and in perfect trim. A terrific cheer from the glider pilots greeted this, and the party went on.

When I got to bed after the party I didn't fall asleep immediately. Perhaps it was the atmosphere of the nearly empty hut. I began to think backwards for the first time. Odd things occurred to me, not particularly important things, and in no special order. The life we had led at Arnhem was nearer to animal existence than anything we could have conceived, and yet the more savage the fighting got, the more civilised the men seemed to become. By civilised I don't mean having baths and being clean and shaving and eating with a knife and fork, but the relations between man and man. They became increasingly polite and helpful. There was such gentleness and friendship among them as would have made any of them almost uncomfortable back on the station. Although they were fighting like tigers, and in that fight had to be completely ruthless, there was no tough behaviour or coarseness of speech. It was almost uncanny. The familiar army swear words and idiom were absent from their conversation, probably for the first time since any of them joined the service. They were courteous, kind and considerate, without any self-consciousness. I remembered the awful moment when I had had to admit that it was I who had thrown those grenades into the next house. Ten days before, if I had trodden on the toe of one of those men, a stream of filthy abuse would have been hurled at me. Now, all they did was to point out politely and with no recriminations, that I wasn't very clever. I remembered Cooper being shot by the Pole, and the quiet way he and the others took it and even felt sorry for the weeping soldier who had wounded him. Then the withdrawal in single file, no pushing or jostling; and the complete self-control of the men crouching in the mud, waiting for the boats; the way they passed the lightly wounded to the front. Their concern for the Dutch civilians, and the complete absence of grumbling and bitterness. That is what I call civilised behaviour.

Then I remembered some of the German troops at Arnhem; the continuous shouting and whining, which, even if one hadn't understood it, gave the impression of savagery. Their lack of self-discipline, their desire to get out of everything and not be the one to carry the baby: 'Why send me? Let him do it' or 'Do it yourself.' From my attic, I actually saw a German officer take off his hat and stamp on it in desperation and rage, when his men were quibbling about who should go forward against our positions. I later realised that these were non-combatant troops rounded up to serve in an emergency.

I began to think about what we had talked of among ourselves when we weren't actually fighting. How we had admitted without shame when we were frightened, telling each other about our feelings, recounting the incredible deeds of others. Under ordinary conditions, soldiers never stop talking sex: 'Subject normal.' During the whole seven days I was there, it just ceased to be a topic of conversation or enter our minds. Nor did anyone mention home and family. Perhaps this was because we thought that no one knew of our desperate position and there was no need to worry about them worrying. I really don't think any of us thought at all; we were too busy living and we seemed to act almost entirely by instinct. None of us will probably ever be so natural again as we were there. We were completely without inhibitions; there wasn't time for them.

Looking back I realised that I now had a complete picture of all the people who had been there with me. Then I knew that I had a complete picture of myself. The seven days had given me seven years of experience and confidence; I knew what I was like ... Then I went to sleep.

4

WINRICH BEHR'S STORY

While I was in Germany in the summer of 1990 I was invited to a dinner party by a distant relative, Grafin Nona Oeynhausen-Sierstorff, at her country house. I was seated next to a good-looking grey-haired man of roughly my own age. Nona called him 'Teddy Bear' and introduced me as her twice-removed uncle from London. We began talking to each other and soon discovered that we had both been in the battle of Arnhem. 'Teddy' was Major Winrich Behr, third staff officer under General Krebs, and had been based in the German headquarters in the Hartenstein Hotel at Oosterbeek. Within hours of the British landing, these headquarters became ours.

When we talked I became more and more fascinated as I learnt about the German view of the battle. Then – over 45 years ago – I had, of course, no idea of what the Allied overall strategy was, nor of the reasons for our defeat at Arnhem. I asked Teddy to tell me more about himself and everything he could remember about the battle.

We didn't want to bore the other guests, so we agreed to continue our discussions at another meeting, and to write to each other.

I learnt that he had been born in Berlin on 22 January, 1918, and had been christened Winrich Hans Hubertus Behr. He came from a long line of Prussian army officers and civil servants. His father, sword in hand, had led his regiment into the first great battle of the First World War at Maubeuge. He had been seriously wounded and had retired with the rank of Colonel. Winrich had been brought up by his well-to-do family in the Tiergarten district of Berlin. When the Nazis came to power in 1933 he was a schoolboy of fifteen and became fired by the new political ideas and the National Socialist propaganda. They had promised to ensure that Germany would break free from the disgrace of the Versailles Peace Treaty; they would put and end to unemployment and political corruption, and would establish a firm regime based on law and order. The Hitler-Youth, to which most of Winrich's school friends belonged, with its smart uniforms, its feeling of togetherness and belonging, and its adventurous out-of-door activities, strongly appealed to him. His father, however, categorically forbade him to join. Colonel Behr was a staunch conservative and had supported Hugenberg's German National Party (Deutsche National Partei) which, although it had helped to get the National Socialists into power, was banned by them as soon as Hitler became Chancellor. Winrich's father was a staunch anti-Nazi and totally opposed to 'that bricklayers' apprentice, Adolf Hitler.' But in 1935 the entire youth section of the tennis club, in which Winrich was one of the top players, was forcibly incorporated into the Hitler Youth and he found himself a member of the Nazi cadet party in spite of his father's objections. The same year he passed his final examinations at the French Grammar School. This was followed by six months' compulsory service in the Arbeitsdienst ('labour service' – a work battalion), before he joined an armoured regiment near Potsdam for his basic military training. He was soon transferred to the Military School in Munich, where he was commissioned in January, 1938.

In the spring of that year he took part in the occupation of Czechoslovakia and in the autumn of 1939 in the invasion of Poland. Only then did he realise that Hitler might lead Germany into a full-scale European war. He hoped that such a disaster might be averted, however – perhaps through an understanding with the British, who had always seemed to approve of Hitler's European military adventures, and had even been a party to the dismemberment of Czechoslovakia.

But Britain and France declared war. Poland was conquered very quickly, danger from the east having been averted in August when Hitler signed a very opportunistic treaty with Stalin. Russia was now no threat and Behr became one of the thousands of troops transferred to the western front in 1940. He was appointed commander of a tank company with the rank of Captain and was part of the triumphant drive through Holland, Belgium and France which ended with the French agreeing to an armistice and the remnants of the British Army escaping from Dunkirk.

In the bitter winter of 1941 Behr's Panzer Reconnaissance Unit was sent ahead by train to Naples and then to the welcome sunshine of Tripoli in North Africa. As soon as they landed they were despatched at full speed to el Agheila to join Rommel's Afrika Korps. They arrived in time to take part in the triumphant advance through Tobruk and Benghazi and on via Sollum and Halfaya Pass, well beyond the frontiers of Egypt. The company was employed as a reconnaissance unit, probing ahead of the main army in fast light tanks and reporting back the positions and strengths of the British armour. Often Behr was reporting directly to Rommel. He was very impressed by the Field-Marshal's leadership and his military skill; he also found him a warm and understanding human being.

Behr's operations were so successful that Rommel decorated him with the *Ritterkreuz*, the Knight's Cross, Germany's highest military decoration; he had already been awarded the Iron Cross Second Class in Poland in 1939, and the Iron Cross First Class in France in 1940. At this time in the desert Behr could still believe in a final German victory. Their tanks and armament were superior to those of the British and for a time they even had air superiority. Both sides fought honourably and well and scrupulously observed the Geneva Convention in the treatment of prisoners of war. Behr spent some time talking to British prisoners, finding that they too believed in a final victory, although there was general agreement that war was a horrible and futile activity.

By August of 1942, however, the tide had clearly turned for the Afrika Korps and they began a slow retreat westwards towards Tobruk. The British had been receiving substantial reinforcements of men and equipment and, even more importantly, had a new and brilliant Commander-in-Chief Montgomery.

Behr did not have to experience the ultimate humiliating defeat of the Afrika Korps and its expulsion from North Africa. In his last reconnaissance his unit was surprised by a squadron of the new American Sherman tanks. They managed to get away, but not without taking several direct hits. With shrapnel in his chest and upper arms, Behr was flown out to Germany and a military hospital. His convalescence was followed by an undemanding job as an instructor in a military school near Potsdam. This quiet life lasted only a short time and then he was assigned to the Sixth Army, commanded by General von Paulus, at that moment fighting the Russian army on the Eastern Front. In October, 1942, he joined the staff of the Sixth Army Headquarters in Golubinka on the River Don, about 30 miles west of Stalingrad. There Behr found himself in charge of artillery, as well as being responsible for keeping up-to-date maps of the military situation and for dealing with all incoming and outgoing reports on the progress of the battle that was raging at Stalingrad.

The great Russian attack began on 20 November. Behr and Oberst Elchlepp, the first general staff officer, flew the next day in a Fieseler Storch reconnaissance aircraft to Gumrak, the nearest landing-strip to Stalingrad. From there they made their way on foot through the thunder and smoke of the barrage until they reached General Paulus's bunker, where they helped to organise the communications. Behr reported daily to Paulus on the general situation in Stalingrad – a situation that became more desperate each day.

With the onset of the Russian winter, hunger, disease and the bitter cold began to take a greater toll than the relentless bombardment from the encircling Russian armies. And still the Führer's orders were to hold on to their positions and then counter-attack. They knew the situation was hopeless, but Hitler and his General Staff would take no notice of their desperate pleas either for reinforcements or for permission to surrender. On 13 January, 1943, Paulus ordered Behr to fly out to report in person to Hitler in the Wolfsschanze – the 'Wolf's Lair'. Paulus said that Hitler had lost all faith in his generals: he hoped that he might listen instead to an 'ordinary', though highly decorated, tank officer.

Behr's plane took off in the late afternoon, just before the airfield fell into Russian hands. He landed in Taganrog near the Black Sea, reported to Field-Marshal von Manstein and, on the morning of the 14th, flew to East Prussia. That evening he reported to Hitler's head-quarters, and there met the Führer and his General Staff for three and a half hours. All the top generals were there – Field-Marshal Keitel, commanding the Wehrmacht, Colonel-General Jodl, Head of Operations, Major-General Schmundt, Hitler's Chief Adjutant, and Martin Bormann, Hitler's Deputy.

Captain Behr presented an extremely clear picture of the situation facing the encircled armies in Russia. The Germans were under continuous bombardment; the cold was intense – some 30 degrees Celsius below zero; there was no shelter and no transport – even the pack horses had been eaten, Behr wanted to know what help they could expect. This was the first time Hitler had heard the truth about Stalingrad. He seemed stunned, then responded with a rapid outline of his plans for an offensive to start in six weeks. He complained bitterly about all the mistakes that had been made and detailed the situation in the various sectors, but he did not breathe a word about support, or supplies, or reinforcements. Behr was unable to remain silent. In spite of himself, he interrupted Hitler. The army, he said, was at the end of its strength: it was essential that he could tell them what supplies they could expect within the next 48 hours: that was all the time they had left. No one had ever interrupted the Führer before. There was dead silence. Everyone expected an explosion, but none came. Hitler remained calm, and quietly ordered Field-Marshal Milch of the Luftwaffe to look into the possibility of supplying help from the air. The conference was over. And Behr was now convinced that the war was lost.

Behr was lucky. He had to stay at Hitler's headquarters because there were now no more flights to the Eastern Front. But the thought of the helpless suffering of his comrades in Stalingrad hung over him like a dead weight and he was unable to rejoice in his own escape. In the comparative peace and luxury of the Wolfschanze he followed the disastrous news from Stalingrad hour by hour. He wondered how much longer they could hold out. They lasted another three weeks before Field-Marshal Paulus (he was promoted in one of Hitler's last orders to the beleaguered garrison) surrendered with seven other generals and 45,000 officers and men. In the whole Stalingrad operation 200,000 Germans were killed and some 100,000 taken prisoner, of whom fewer than 4000 managed to get back to Germany after the war.

After Stalingrad, Behr was posted to command an infantry battalion in the Caucasus, where he served for seven months; then, promoted to the rank of Major in the General Staff – with an impressive red stripe down his trousers – he was attached as staff officer to Army Group 'B' in northern France, first at Fontainebleau and then at La Roche Guyon on the Seine. Here he was pleased to be reporting once again directly to Rommel. But he found the Field-Marshal greatly changed; he was in poor health, and lacked his former drive and warmth of feeling. (Later, in suspicious circumstances, Rommel committed suicide, having been badly wounded in France in July, 1944.) Behr was then responsible successively to Field-Marshal von Kluge, General Krebs, and, finally, Field-Marshal Model. It was as First Assistant Staff Officer to General Krebs that Behr took part in the Battle of Arnhem, an impression of which the German point of view is given in the next chapter. He remained with Model until the very end, trying to save as many men and as much material as possible during the retreat of German armies in North-West Europe, following the Allied invasion of France in June, 1944.

In December, 1944, Hitler ordered a massive offensive, under the overall command of Field-Marshal von Rundstedt, through the Ardennes Forest in Belgium which, he claimed, would finally stop the retreat by breaking the Allied front in the west and cutting their supply lines. Model still believed in the Führer and in the possibility of a German victory, and threw himself enthusiastically into the planning of this daring project. Behr had no such faith, but gave Model his full co-operation and stayed by his side throughout the ensuing 'Battle of the Bulge'. When, by the middle of January, 1945, it was clear that the battle was lost, Model committed suicide and Major Behr changed into civilian clothes and went home to join his family.

As soon as he could after the end of the war, Winrich Behr went to Bonn University and then to Frankfurt, where he studied law. He qualified as a lawyer in Dusseldorf in 1952, and was then recruited by Jean Monnet, the founder of the European Coal and Fuel Community – the forerunner of the European Common Market – and in time became head of the private office of the Deputy President. He was called to Brussels by his former teacher, Professor Doctor Walther Hallstein, and there became Deputy General Secretary of the EEC. In 1965 he was appointed Managing Director of Telefonbau and Normalzeit, a business manufacturing private telephones and switchboards. Then it had a turnover of 400 million Deutschmarks and employed 12,000 people. When Winrich Behr retired in 1983 the turnover had increased to 2.3 billion marks.

In his lovely country house near Düsseldorf he is very busy – he is on the board of several industrial concerns and on committees concerned with Prussian country houses and gardens, and European cultural institutions. He describes himself as a European – but he is actually a very admirable citizen of the world.

5

THE GERMAN VIEW
OF THE BATTLE

Sunday

On this sunny Sunday morning, while Louis Hagen was sitting in the NAAFI canteen on Windrush airfield in East Anglia, waiting to hear when his glider section would be despatched to Holland, Major Winrich Behr, first assistant staff officer to General Krebs, the Chief of Staff, had just finished his lunch in the Hotel Hartenstein in the suburb of Oosterbeek, 2 miles west of the town of Arnhem. It was a beautiful day and he was enjoying an unaccustomed and very welcome feeling of relaxation.

For more than three months, since the Allied invasion of Normandy on 6 June, 1944, the Germans had been steadily pushed back across Europe by an enemy with greatly superior armour and firepower. Their slow and bloody retreat out of France, through Belgium and into Holland, had at last come to a halt. It seemed that their dogged and relentless pursuers had finally run out of steam. They now had three major rivers between them and the enemy; Behr felt it was about time for a quiet breathing space.

He had had a long and exciting war: he had won his Ritterkreuz with Rommel in North Africa and had been one of the last officers to escape from the frozen shambles of Stalingrad. His present situation was almost routine compared with his previous experiences.

But there was much to do. All round Arnhem the Germans had set up a series of field workshops and transit camps where the stragglers and survivors of the long retreat could be collected together. Many divisions had been reduced to a fraction of their original strength and were now being regrouped into new operational units. Every day specialised freight trains brought back the battered tanks and mobile guns which had stubbornly held back the Allied advance, allowing the infantry and other troops to fall back towards Germany. Here in relative peace the fitters and engineers worked on urgent repairs and refitting; the weapons were repaired or replaced and the crews re-equipped and retrained. Then, as soon as the tanks, self-propelled guns and fighting vehicles were ready for action, they were sent eastwards without delay to help in the defence of Germany.

There was an enormous concentration of heavy armour in all stages of preparation, from cannibalised wrecks to fully battle-ready Tigers. Some of these were the updated Royal Tigers, with much thicker armour-plating and larger guns, which had proved a match for the Russian T34s. Among its armament was the 88-mm gun (originally an anti-aircraft weapon) that had wrought such havoc among the British tanks in North Africa. The Hotel Tafelberg, also in Oosterbeek and close to the Hartenstein, was the headquarters of Generalfeldmarschall Walter Model; commanding Army Group B. Winrich Behr's immediate boss, Krebs, was his Chief of Staff and was based in the Hotel Feldberg nearby. Model, a typical heavily built professional soldier in the Prussian tradition – he even wore a monacle – had succeeded Generalfeldmarschall Gerd von Rundstedt on

5 September in command of all the German armies between the Dutch coast and Alsace-Lorraine.

Major Behr's quiet lunch was suddenly shattered by the roar of a squadron of fighter-bombers sweeping over the hotel, guns firing. There was a shocked silence and then a babble of excited discussion; the officers present quickly realised that the aircraft had not been firing at them; although in the next room the Staff Artillery Officer, Oberleutnant von Metzsch, had had his soup spoon shot out of his hand.

There had been no preliminary warning of any expected offensive, but the considerable number of aircraft involved strongly indicated that something unpleasant was brewing. Major Behr was suddenly aware of extraordinary goings-on outside the window. He couldn't really believe it, but there, not much more than 300 yards from the hotel, a group of parachutists was silently floating down.

While everyone scrambled to get their weapons, Behr sent a couple of soldiers up to the roof to report what they could see. His first thought was that this was a commando raid aimed at capturing some or all of the senior officers. As well as the Generalfeldmarschall and Krebs, there were at least three other senior generals in the neighbourhood. Behr hurried off to the Feldberg Hotel to report to Krebs.

Some three miles to the north-west, in the Wolfheze Hotel, Sturmbannführer Hans Kraft watched appalled as a mass of gliders silently swept out of the sky. His SS Panzer-Grenadier Training and Depot Battalion, being composed largely of reluctant teenagers and elderly conscripts, were hardly crack front-line troops, but he had no time to worry about that. He rushed out into the courtyard and yelled for all ranks, including trainees and wounded, to grab their weapons and ammunition and take up action stations; the men nervously scurried to and fro. Kraft telephoned his superior, Obergruppenführer Wilhelm Bittrich, commanding II SS Panzer Corps, who told him that there were also reports of airborne troops dropping near Oosterbeek. He ordered Kraft to turn his headquarters into a defended strong-point and to send out armed patrols to find out what the enemy were doing. Reinforcements would be sent as soon as possible.

When Major Behr reached the Tafelberg Hotel he found that Krebs had already received reports of glider landings and that Model was hurriedly packing and had ordered the entire General Staff to move out to Bittrich's headquarters in Deotinchem, some 20 miles to the east.

General Krebs told Behr to find out if there were any enemy troops to the north or east of Arnhem and to prepare transport. Behr rushed back to the Hartenstein, where the men from the roof reported that they had seen a mass of planes, troop- and cargo-carrying gliders, and parachutists, mostly to the west and north of the town.

Somewhat to Behr's surprise, all the telephone lines were open and the roads back to the east were clear. Immediate preparations were made to evacuate. By this time they were so used to the routine of sudden departures that there was no undue excitement. During the past six months they had had to move their headquarters so many times that there were now comparatively few secret documents or codes to burn. It was really no more than a matter of packing up shaving kit and spare clothes and piling into the waiting transport.

Within half an hour Behr was in his BMW staff car, driving away from Arnhem as part of a convoy headed by Model in his bullet-proof personnel carrier, with an escort of four light tanks.

Back at Wolfheze, Sturmbannführer Kraft's patrols were reporting that several hundred enemy soldiers had landed and were being mar-shalled into columns, apparently preparing to move into the town. Pleased by the response of his untried young troops, Kraft sent a larger group with mortars and anti-tank guns to attack the troops in the landing area. Other groups he told to get ahead of the invaders on the road to Oosterbeek and set up ambushes and strong-points to impede them as much as possible.

Doetinchem was where Obergruppenführer Bittrich had set up his corps' logistic headquarters. He was a good-looking regular officer who had joined the Waffen SS as a tactical career move, without having any kind of commitment to National Socialism. Bittrich was the overall area commander; his troops included the surviving units of the 9th SS (Hohenstaufen) Panzer Division and the 10th SS (Frundsberg) Panzer Division. He had been warned of the imminent arrival of the Generalfeldmarschall and his staff and gave instructions for accommodation to be found in houses and farms nearby.

Bittrich now began to prepare the counter-attack. He ordered Obersturmbannführer Walter Harzer, 9th SS Panzer's chief of staff and temporary commander, to send a reconnaissance group in some strength to check out the country between Arnhem and Nijmegen to the south, and to secure the bridge over the Waal in the latter town. He wanted another force to occupy Arnhem, reinforce the guard at the bridge and hold it until Brigadeführer Heinz Harmel's 10th SS Panzer could take over the responsibility. Once the bridge was secure and handed over to the men from the Frundsberg Division, the Hohenstaufen panzers were to destroy the enemy forces near Oosterbeek.

The 9th SS Panzer Division had been refitting for the past three or four weeks in their staging-post near Apeldoorn. Recently Harzer had been told to transfer several of his tanks and armoured cars to Harmel's Frundsberg Division, which was in a much weaker state, and which had been ordered back to Berlin. Harzer had decided to keep back some of his tanks, however, and the workshops had accordingly been told to remove tracks or wheels from those in best condition and then report them unserviceable. Now, following the Obergruppenführer's orders, the tanks had quickly to be put back into fighting order. But on this lovely September Sunday most of the men were off duty. Twenty trucks were sent to quarter the town picking up any 9th Panzer men they saw and to tell all the others to pass on the word for all ranks to join in the defence of the town, making their way to wherever they heard shooting. Although the engineers and fitters worked with record speed, it was not till late afternoon that a sufficient number of tanks were battle-ready.

Harzer had now divided his division into two groups (Kampfgruppen), and given Sturmbannführer Brinkmann responsibility for checking the road to Nijmegen while Sturmbannführer Spindler was to hold the bridge, occupy Arnhem and deal with the forces at Oosterbeek. It was late afternoon before Spindler's group drove into Arnhem and reported that the town was deserted.

Shortly afterwards Brinkmann's 40-vehicle reconnaissance force drove over the bridge towards Nijmegen.

As all was quiet at the bridge, Spindler decided to drive on to where the action was. Beyond the St Elizabeth hospital there was a lot of shelling and machine-gun fire: the invading force was being held up by Kraft's battling teenagers from the training battalion, reinforced by stray soldiers alerted by the 9th SS Panzer trucks when they were rounding up their troops. Spindler left four tanks to reinforce the defenders and with the rest of his group he set up barricades across the two main roads leading from Oosterbeek into Arnhem. Harzer also sent another group from the Hohenstaufen Panzers to guard the roads from Ede and Utrecht. Model, meanwhile, had set up his new headquarters in a little castle in the town of Terborg, about 5 miles away from Doetinchem. Reports from Arnhem were continually arriving there, and Model called a staff meeting to evaluate the situation. It was soon clear that there was no danger of any immediate breakthrough in strength. All the reports coming in showed that there were more than enough troops and armour in and around Arnhem to deal with the enemy threat – whatever their intentions might be.

So what were the enemy up to? The possibility of a raid on his headquarters had very quickly been discounted: it had been perfect dropping weather with a very light breeze, so they had to assume that the obviously experienced parachutists were dropping where they had meant to drop. In which case the main force had landed too far away from the General Headquarters to mount a surprise attack.

For the same reasons, Model insisted that the road bridge could not have been the target. A complete brigade dropped as close to the southern end of the bridge as the soft ground allowed could have overcome the small guard posts and held the bridge against determined opposition for a significant length of time. But from the reports it was clear that all the fighting had been on the outskirts of the town and that no troops had dropped anywhere near the road or rail bridges.

What did that leave? An attempt to destroy the regrouping Panzer brigades? This was one of the earlier theories, and a number of nearly battle-ready Tiger tanks had quickly been loaded on to two trains, ready to pull out to the east. But as no sign of the enemy's interest in the tank repair workshops had developed, the trains were unloaded and the Tigers returned to their workshops.

The headquarters staff assumed that the enemy would have had complete intelligence about the concentration of armour round Arnhem. All the activities connected with moving and repairing heavy tanks could not have been hidden from the local population, some of whom were undoubtedly in touch with the Dutch underground. And however carefully they camouflaged their workshops, the enemy's air reconnaissance must have revealed the tell-tale signs of continuous tank movements. But again, the force that had landed was much too small to engage and destroy the German armour; a squadron of heavy bombers would have been much more appropriate. The only possible explanation was that the landings were a diversion intended to keep a large number of troops and armour engaged with the airborne forces while a surprise ground attack took place somewhere else.

At Model's HQ Winrich Behr could not spend too much time on speculation. The myriad administrative details with flowed from their sudden move would keep him busy for several days. In a cramped little office at the top of the castle he reached for the telephone to start linking up with the local authorities and services, informing everyone who might need to know where he and General Krebs were now operating.

Bittrich tracked down the Generalfeldmarschall in his new head-quarters in Terborg and outlined his plans, which Model immediately approved. Meanwhile reports had come in of heavy fighting against American airborne troops near Nijmegen and Eindhoven, and Model now said that he was sure that the ultimate objective of the drop was the Ruhr. All their energies should be devoted to blocking any moves by the enemy to break out in a north-easterly direction. Bittrich argued that, in that case, surely they should now blow the bridges at Arnhem and Nijmegen. Model absolutely refused, however, saying that the bridges were essential for the deployment of German armour.

Back in Arnhem, there was intermittent firing all night as Spindler's force attacked pockets of enemy troops along both sides of the rail-way, and at the north end of the bridge.

Monday

Early in the morning the reconnaissance group from Harzer's 9th SS Panzer returned from Nijmegen where they had had a sharp engage-ment with an American force holding one of the two bridges over the Waal. They had driven them off with few losses and were return-ing to join up with the rest of the division. They drove unsuspectingly straight over Arnhem bridge, only to be met with enemy small-arms and anti-tank fire: overnight the north end of the bridge had been captured by the British airborne troops. Four scout cars had raced across and into the town before they were blown up. Eight half-track vehicles following were destroyed on the bridge and the rest of the group quickly reversed to the shelter of the south bank.

Sturmbannführer Kraft had been warned to expect another land-ing further west of Wolfheze. When his patrols reported enemy troops defending the Groote Heide, an area of heathland where the most westerly of the British DZs was, he sent out three groups with machine-guns to deal with them. There followed a continuous exchange of fire with casualties on both sides, enlivened at one point by a Luftwaffe squadron dropping a carpet of bombs on the open space between the combatants. And shortly after that came an even more worrying event – the arrival of the anticipated landing. Suddenly the sky was filled with hundreds of gliders and parachutists.* To Kraft's teenagers from the Panzer Training Brigade, the sky seemed to be blotted out by a thousand parachutes. They knew that this was no place for them and hurried back to Wolfheze.

Obergruppenführer Bittrich was alarmed when he heard Kraft's report on the size of the enemy landings. He felt very much under pressure. He was still waiting for the promised reinforcements under Generalleutnant Hans von Tettau, whose scratch 'division' had been stationed on the River Waal to collect stragglers from the fighting on the Maas and re-form them into fighting units, and was now to the west of Arnhem. Bittrich now ordered Kraft to send his entire force to join up with Spindler's group from 9th SS Panzer, which was already fighting in the town itself. There the north end of the road bridge was held by the enemy,** due to the inexplicable negligence of Harzer who had been told specifically to hold the bridge until relieved by 10th SS Panzer. Now it was going to be very difficult to get the tanks from 10th Panzer over to the south bank of the river where they would be needed to deal with any further enemy landings in the Nijmegen area. Bittrich therefore told Harmel that he would now have to ferry his division across the river at Pannerden, 7½ miles south-east of Arnhem. But it would be a slow business.

---

* The second pilot in one of the gliders approaching the landing-zone at Wolfheze was Louis Hagen.

** This was a force from 1 Parachute Brigade under Lieutenant-Colonel John Frost, mainly Frost's own 2nd Battalion Parachute Regiment. As they had advanced from their LZ into Arnhem, the railway bridge was demolished just as they reached it, and they found the pontoon bridge partially dismantled. The road bridge was thus the only practicable crossing for miles.

Tuesday

Now that the scale of the enemy operations seemed to be clearer, Model moved his headquarters back to just north of Arnhem, where Harzer had his command post in the Heseburgherweg School. By now von Tettau had arrived with an ad hoc fighting force of administrative and training units, an SS depot battalion, an NCOs' School and a battalion of Dutch SS men, and was ordered by Bittrich to guard the area of the landing-zones to the north-west of Oosterbeek. Von Tettau found these in the control of the Allied airborne troops and sent Standartenführer Lippert (the CO of the NCOs' School) with six old Renault tanks and a company of infantry to clear them out. The tanks with their untrained crews were swiftly dealt with by British Piat anti-tank weapons. But, following a feint attack by Lippert, the scratch German infantry charged the airborne defenders, put them to flight and pursued them towards Arnhem.

When Lippert returned to the landing-zone he found that a large parachute and glider landing had taken place and has great difficulty getting back to von Tettau's headquarters, although he managed to round up a few dozen British prisoners on the way.

Wednesday

At dawn the heavy SS Frundsberg Mortar Section moved into position and blasted the Arnhem bridgehead. This was followed by a frontal attack by ten somewhat elderly tanks firing wildly but continuously, and supported by infantry keeping up a steady pounding of heavy machine-gun fire. The tanks were met by the very accurate fire of the British 6-pounder anti-tank guns; they slowed, came to a stop and then began to back away. The barrage quietened and the machine-gunners slipped back with the tanks. But, from a safer distance, the SS mortars kept up a continuous fire.

Reinforcements continued to pour into the battle area. Model could now report to Hitler that the larger part of the Fifteenth Army in the Antwerp area, which Montgomery's forces had by-passed during their advance, leaving it to escape largely intact, had now crossed the Scheldt and were in a position to move against the enemy near Nijmegen. Here the narrow corridor of enemy transport was also being attacked by II Parachute Corps from the Reichswald Forest.

There was an immediate and unexpected gain from the fighting round Nijmegen. Allied battle plans had been found on the body of an American officer whose glider had crashed near the town. They included details of an imminent new landing at the village of Johannahoeve, west of Arnhem but east of Wolfheze. Model ordered Kraft's SS Panzer-Grenadier Training and Reserve Battalion to surround the landing-zone.

They found enemy troops already there and immediately engaged them. The battle was at its fiercest when the landings started; the luckless glider and parachute troops dropped in the midst of the fighting and many were killed as they landed.

Thursday

It was a time of almost total confusion with no clear line of separation between the two forces. It seemed as though there were three distinct battles. Elements of 10th SS Panzer were attacking the British forces holding the north end of the Arnhem road bridge, Kraft's training battalion, with reinforcements from 9th SS Panzer, were doing their best to block three separate thrusts from the west by airborne troops desperate to relieve the forces holding the bridge. Here, between the Rhine and the centre of Arnhem, British troops were doggedly fighting their way towards the bridge street by street, and were suffering considerably in the process.

The invading force's headquarters was now in the Hotel Hartenstein in Oosterbeek, and the third battle involved 9th SS Panzer, which had formed a ring of armour round this headquarters perimeter and were subjecting the enemy to a continuous artillery barrage. The fighting in the western suburbs and the Oosterbeek area was even closer and more concentrated than elsewhere, with the Germans sometimes occupying houses next door to those held by the enemy.* In some cases the opposing sides even found themselves on different floors of the same house.

Model was annoyed and worried: he could not understand how it was possible for the tiny British force still to be holding the Arnhem bridgehead, thus preventing the German heavy armour moving south where they would be needed to start clearing the area around Nijmegen. He told Bittrich in uncompromising terms to get something done about it. Harzer was to use whatever forces were needed and free the bridgehead within 24 hours.

To help the operation Model ordered the evacuation of all civilians from Arnhem and told the Luftwaffe to mount a heavy bombing raid on the town centre. Convoys of lorries and ambulances took out the women and children. 9th SS Panzer were made responsible for the collection and assembly of the many enemy prisoners, and also the wounded of both sides.

The bombers pounded the already wrecked city centre, making house-to-house fighting more difficult for both sides. By evening the Dutch police, firemen, air-raid wardens, doctors and nurses were the only civilians left in Arnhem.

Meanwhile the fighting round the bridgehead had reached a new intensity. Many of the defended buildings were on fire and the British wounded were in danger of being burnt alive. Under the protection of white flags, officers of 9th SS Panzer agreed with the British officer in charge, Major Freddie Gough** – whose senior, Colonel Frost, had

---

* In one of these Louis Hagen was fighting from an attic window with a Piat and a Bren-gun.
** Gough in fact commanded 1st Airborne Division's Reconnaissance Squadron, some elements of which had reached the bridge.

been wounded – to a temporary cease-fire while the casualties were rescued from the burning houses.

But the battle of the bridgehead was nearly at an end. That night the intensive pounding of the British positions at the bridge by the Kampfgruppe Brinkmann artillery reached a climax. There was very little response coming from the trapped British troops.

Friday

On the Friday morning things were looking a lot better to Obergruppenführer Bittrich. The first news was that the bridgehead had been finally captured and that Major Knaust with eight Panther tanks had swept aside the wrecks of the vehicles that had been destroyed on the bridge and was racing south to join the fighting at Nijmegen. Most of the remaining enemy forces were now corralled in a small enclave round the Hartenstein Hotel in Oosterbeek, and German reinforcements had been flowing in from all points of the compass – a motley collection of units ranging from battle-hardened tank men to sixteen-year-old 'non combatants'. Hauptsturmführer von Allworden reported with a unit from the SS Panzer Pursuit Corps, and Obersturmbannführer Harder with an SS Panzer Company. And Bittrich had another stroke of luck. Full details of the proposed landing-zones for a new supply drop had been found in a crashed British glider. So when Harzer got news of a further airborne force crossing the coast at Dunkirk – a large force with many heavy transport aircraft travelling south-east, clearly making for Arnhem – Bittrich was ready. He ordered a general alert and warned Spindler to increase the number of troops guarding the proposed landing-zones, which the British had already marked with large coloured rectangles for different kinds of stores, as detailed in the captured plans. His task was made easier because the 503rd Panzer Division had just arrived with an additional 45 Royal Tiger tanks. Also a panzer-grenadier battalion from Berlin was unloading at the rail terminal.

At the landing-zones anti-aircraft guns were prepared for action, everyone waiting for the expected arrival time – 1600 hours. The tension grew; then the Luftwaffe gave the first indication of the arrival of the airborne force. A squadron of German fighters roared over the town, immediately splitting up as escorting enemy fighters rushed in to head them off. The anti-aircraft guns pounded the skies as the black mass of planes neared the town. Small-arms and machine-gun fire joined in. The slowly descending transport planes and parachutes dropped helplessly into a waiting inferno.

The German troops surrounding the landing-zone soon realised that most of the parachutes were marked with red and white stripes. They knew that this meant that they were bearing supplies, not armed soldiers. Gradually the firing died down and the men watched as the Allied planes braved the barrage of flak to drop a rich harvest directly into their enemies' hands. The Germans gained a much appreciated haul of medical supplies, emergency rations, bacon, milk powder, bread, flour, and even chocolate. This 'Father Christmas' drop cost the enemy dearly in crashed planes and dead aircrew.

By now the condition of the wounded – both British and German – within the Hartstein compound was desperate. There was a shortage of drinking water, as well as medical supplies. As a humanitarian gesture Harzer, commander of the 9th SS Panzer Division, sent Hauptsturmführer Doktor Skalka to negotiate a cease-fire and to offer to have all the wounded moved out to hospitals in the town.

Dr Skalka drove into the compound with a British soldier sitting on the bonnet of his car holding a large Red Cross flag. He was met by 1st Airborne Division senior medical officer, Colonel Graeme Warrack, who got Urquhart's permission to accompany Skalka back to 9th SS Panzer headquarters. Arrangements were quickly completed, and as a result a cease-fire was accepted by both sides. A convoy of German ambulances drove into the Allied compound to bring out all the seriously wounded German troops, as well as many British and Polish soldiers. They were distributed among field hospitals in Arnhem, and in the St Elizabeth Hospital which was still staffed by British doctors and orderlies under German supervision.

Saturday

Bittrich now ordered all German forces to concentrate on the pocket of enemy troops centred round Oosterbeek.

At the same time 45 Tiger tanks of 503rd Panzer Division, under von Tettau, with supporting infantry, began attacking the airborne troops who were dug in round the Heveadorp ferry. Many Allied troops were killed or wounded, but by the late afternoon 503rd Panzer had failed to gain any ground.

Harzer's Hohenstaufen tanks were holding the area to the north and Kraft was attacking from Oosterbeek on the east. By the afternoon several streets had been cleared, in spite of desperate defence by the enemy using pistols and hand grenades. There were heavy losses on both sides. Several of the German commanders commented on the incredible bravery of the Allied troops, by now heavily outnumbered and completely outgunned. At dusk the Frundsberg and Hohenstaufen tanks probed into the enemy pocket, enabling snipers to take up positions in trees and empty buildings.

Sunday

Next day tanks from 9th SS Panzer attacked along the northern rim of the Hartenstein perimeter, but were driven off by artillery fire from the south bank of the Rhine – elements of Second Army had at last reached Arnhem, though too late to do much for 1st Airborne. The Germans nicknamed the concentrated pocket of resistance 'Der Hexenkessel' – the witches' cauldron. By now a continuous pall of black smoke hung over the cauldron where the Allied airborne troops were fighting to survive. The acrid stench of high-explosive mixed with the oily reek of burning vehicles. Intermittent flashes of artillery fire and exploding mortar shells only emphasised the surrounding gloom.

Frustrated by the prolonged stalemate, Harzer decided to try a psychological approach. He had loudspeakers set up in the trees round the perimeter; through them, the enemy were told how hopeless their situation was, that no reinforcements could possibly reach them, and that good treatment, food and drink awaited them if they only gave up their useless resistance. These attempts were met with defiant and scornful shouts from the defending airborne troops.

Monday

Next day Bittrich ordered attacks to be redoubled on all sides of the 'cauldron'. He had been pleased to learn that fifteen Royal Tiger tanks were on their way to reinforce 9th SS Panzer on the east of the perimeter. Together with flame throwers from the 9th Pioneer Instructing Battalion, they were now able to overcome individual strong-points in the cauldron. But it was slow work and the Royal Tigers, massive and virtually impregnable, proved unwieldy and awkward in the narrow and rubble-strewn streets of Oosterbeek.

On the eastern side Harzer regrouped the SS Hohenstaufen into four separate spearhead assault groups under Sturmbannführers Mollers, Spindler, von Allworden and Harder. In the afternoon von Allworden and Harder broke through and destroyed two British artillery positions, but were halted from advancing further by artillery fire from elsewhere within the perimeter. Bittrich was now getting reports that the enemy fire seemed to be getting weaker and more sporadic. He passed the good news on to Model, who reported in turn to von Rundstedt (the C-in-C West, and thus Model's immediate superior), telling him that in order to destroy the extremely stubborn enemy he had to have reinforcements, including at least a Panzer brigade with infantry and an artillery battalion.

Meanwhile, more artillery was being brought into action. All the available heavy guns of the 191st Artillery Regiment were targeted on Oosterbeek and then began a continuous and head-splitting barrage over the whole of the seething cauldron. Now, adding to the excruciating din, the Allied artillery on the south bank of the Rhine began a continuous attack on 191st Artillery Regiment's gun positions. This exceptional concentration of fire from the enemy heavy artillery was a worrying development.

Tuesday

Shortly after midnight men of Kampfgruppe Harder reported that several boats had tried to cross from the south bank, but had been driven back or sunk by mortar and rifle fire. Bittrich began to wonder whether the enemy might now be in a position to send in reinforcements, and so turn the troops in the Hartenstein pocket once more into a dangerous attacking force. He ordered Harder to keep a steady mortar barrage over the river and on to the southern bank for the rest of the night.*

At first light Bittrich ordered redoubled attacks on all sides of the smoking and tangled wreckage and ruins that were all that was left of the cauldron. The Hohenstaufen tanks pushed forward, surprised at the thinness of the defending fire. Then, eerily, the firing from within the perimeter seemed to peter out. The sudden silence was unsettling. Gingerly the tanks from the two Kampfgruppen edged their way towards the Hartenstein Hotel, infantry fanning out behind them. The tanks reached the hotel and the infantry circled round it silently. They reached the tennis courts and were suddenly greeted with a chorus of German voices. This was the prisoners' compound, and the Hohenstaufen men now learned that it really was all over. The prisoners told them that the Allied troops had pulled out overnight; all

---

* At about this time Louis Hagen was swimming across the Rhine to safety.

that were left were sick and wounded men who had been firing at random while the main body of defenders escaped across the river.

It was over. The German soldiers couldn't believe it. During all the turmoil of the night's artillery and mortar duel, the apparently invincible airborne fighters – or at least the survivors – had slipped unnoticed across the lower Rhine.

Major Winrich Behr learnt with amazement that the Allied forces that launched the airborne attack, of which Generalfeldmarschall Model had made so light, had fought on for nine days against, among other troops, two elite SS armoured divisions. It had been quite a problem after all, but a problem that had eventually brought its own rewards. The Germans had made enormous gains. Many British officers and thousands of parachute and airborne soldiers had been taken prisoner. In the Arnhem-Oosterbeek area along 9th SS Panzer Brigade had captured some 6000 British and Polish prisoners. The booty had included an arsenal of weapons, ammunition and equipment, including a number of light tanks and anti-tank guns, innumerable jeeps and field howitzers, 250 field weapons of all kinds, 1000 gliders, untold numbers of rifles and other small arms, and an enormous quantity of supplies. Nearly 100 RAF aircraft had been destroyed. And in the course of the nine-day struggle, an elite and highly trained enemy fighting division had been destroyed.

6

SUMMING UP

When I started to write the background to this book, nearly 50 years after its first publication, I read most major accounts of the battle of Arnhem in both the English and the German archives. Gradually I began to understand the overall strategy – and the muddle, the heroism and the waste. Quite apart from the unpredictability of any battle, as well as several strategic errors, I have come to believe that there was one major reason for the British defeat at Arnhem – the overwhelming ambition of Field-Marshal Montgomery. He was a brilliant leader, full of imaginative ideas, but he was an emotionally withdrawn man. He had a reputation as a meticulous strategist who would never move without overwhelming odds in his favour. This time his judgement failed. He resented being subordinate to General Eisenhower and was frustrated by what he saw as the Americans and Russians. His arrogant ambition discounted adverse intelligence reports prior to 'Market Garden', and doubts expressed by senior staff officers.

At first Eisenhower had opposed the plan, but Montgomery's enthusiasm and confidence finally persuaded him to agree. The enormous undertaking was planned in a single week and went ahead under the code-name 'Market Garden'. The British 1st Airborne Division was to lead the attack, supported by Allied ground forces with American airborne troops responsible for taking the bridges south of Arnhem.

The first strategic error was probably in the choice of drop- and landing-zones at Arnhem. Four main ones were chosen (there were two others, and a supply dropping-point) some six miles outside the city. The RAF had advised Montgomery that the Division should not be landed close to the town because of the danger from anti-aircraft fire. But these zones proved to be too far from the Arnhem road bridge, which was the main objective. In the event, only some 700 men out of the whole 10,000 reached the bridge. In balancing the relative risks, Montgomery should have overruled the RAF. As it turned out, the anti-aircraft fire was surprisingly light during the first two major landings.

Montgomery's second error was to agree with the RAF's plan to spread the drop over three days, instead of making two trips in one day. The RAF had not enough aircraft to do the whole operation in one drop and wanted to minimise the strain on aircrew and ground staff that would result from making the same flight twice in one day. The element of surprise was of course lost after the first landing; and the weather then deteriorated. So the second landing was delayed by several hours, and the third by three days. Twenty-four hours after the first landing the Germans had successfully organised their defences.

It was also a mistake to overlook the danger prevented by the fact that the only road available for Second Army's advancing tanks was clearly visible to the German artillery. The Dutch officers who were attached to the General Staff, including Prince Bernhard, could have warned them about this, but they were excluded from the planning sessions. Had they been there, they would also have reported that two

SS Panzer Divisions were refitting near Arnhem. Perhaps the Dutch were excluded because of fear of possible leakage of information to the Dutch Nazis.

The need for good radio communication was underestimated; during the whole battle of Arnhem the equipment proved totally inadequate. It was not suitable for the terrain and was not powerful enough, either for ground-to-ground or ground-to-air communication.

Another factor contributing to the Allied defeat could perhaps not have been foreseen; in spite of their exhausting retreat across Europe, the German army responded to the Allied landings with astonishing resilience, imagination and speed. Montgomery gravely underestimated the quality of his enemy.

But perhaps the most serious error was to land the British invasion force right into the middle of the greatest concentration of German forces on the western front.

Montgomery persisted in his choice of landing at Arnhem in spite of a succession of detailed reports from the active and reliable Dutch Underground, and from Allied air reconnaissance. To Model and his staff it had seemed impossible that the British should not have known what was going on behind the German lines. To Montgomery it was unthinkable that his ambition to be first in Berlin should not be fulfilled. Against the prospect of a dazzling victory, and an end to five years of war, he persuaded himself that the risk of enormous casualties was worth taking. His powers of self-deception did not fail him, even in defeat. Thousands of men were killed or wounded, and thousands more taken prisoner; hundres of aircraft were lost; and the Allied armies were unable to advance into Germany for another four months.

Yet Montgomery's comment was that the operation was '90 per cent' successful; he remained, he wrote, 'an unrepentant advocate of "Market Garden"'.

7

LIFE AFTER ARNHEM

The morning after I got back to England, Wing-Commander Lillywhite, CO of the airfield, called me into his office. He told me that I had been awarded the Military Medal for 'bravery in the field', and that I was to be decorated by the King at Buckingham Palace. He then mentioned a slight problem – my unmilitary bearing and sloppy uniform. 'It would not fit the occasion. In fact,' he said, 'it's a tragedy that the only man on the airfield to be decorated is a scarecrow like you.' He suggested that after my two weeks' survivor's leave I should report to the Guards Brigade at Wellington Barracks, near Buckingham Palace, to be smartened up and to learn the correct drill for the investiture.

I had never heard of the Military Medal and could not imagine how anyone in London could have known about what I had done at Arnhem a few days earlier. Later I learnt that it was Captain Ogilvie – the 'Captain Z' of *Arnhem Lift* – who had sent a radio message from the HQ at Oosterbeek recommending me for the award. I was deeply upset to learn that he had been drowned crossing the Rhine: he was a really good man, warm-hearted, and with a great sense of humour. I left Commander Lillywhite in a happy daze – ahead of me I had my survivor's leave and several more weeks in London as well.

And now, wherever I went, friends asked me what had happened at Arnhem. I got so bored repeating the story that I thought I had better write it all down and get it duplicated. The girlfriend I was staying with became most enthusiastic about the idea, but I soon got tired of it. She was determined, however, and devised a regime by which I was only allowed the necessities of my life – love and food – when I had completed five typed pages. I tried to fool her by enlarging the margins and increasing the spacing of the lines, but she always found out. In this way we completed a 150-page report in two weeks. She was still enthusiastic and thought it should be published.

For this I had to submit my story to my Commanding Officer, Colonel Murray. He was outraged. 'You should be ashamed of ourself!' he said, 'No Britisher would ever have let his comrades down by writing stuff like this. It lets down the whole regiment! I won't even pass it to the War Office. I forbid you to contact either a publisher or anyone from the press.' He concluded, 'Sergeant Haig, I am very disappointed in you – you of all people, a holder of the Military Medal.'

But my determined girlfriend sent her copy to the War Office without telling me. It was passed for publication, with the proviso that anything in it that might indicate that the author was German had to be cut out. But I had no idea how things were going to work out because Colonel Murray – obviously too ashamed to keep me under his command – had me transferred to a Glider Pilot Regiment unit in India.

Before I left (at the very end of 1944) I had to attend the investiture at Buckingham Palace. There a tall, elderly, most elegantly turned-out major-domo in a frock coat inspected us to make sure we were properly dressed. I was escorted through an antechamber to a large arched double door that led into the ballroom where the investiture was taking place. I was gently pushed through the door.

As smartly as I could, I marched the long distance across the parquet floor, my heavy army boots echoing through the hall. I halted, stamping my feet noisily, and saluted in front of the King, just as the Guards corporal at Wellington Barracks had taught me. With the King were the Queen and their two young daughters, the Princesses Elizabeth and Margaret. They all shook my hand. Then an equerry handed the King a large silver medal on a velvet cushion. He pinned it to my chest and congratulated me. 'And where do you come from?' he asked me, and, before I could think it over, I answered, 'Potsdam, Sir!' The King stammered out something I couldn't understand. Then, after an awkward pause whilst his jaw moved without a sound coming out of his mouth, he continued, 'Arnhem – a terrible tragedy – so many men. But I am sure you are keen to get out there again soon.' I was mesmerised by the struggle the poor man had to get his words out, and before I knew what I was saying, answered, 'No, Sir. I only just got safely back!'

From the look in his eyes I realised the interview was over. I stamped my feet, saluted and marched out of the hall. Later my friends told me that the Queen had stared fixedly at me, plainly wondering how a German had come to be in her drawing room.

I was very upset about being sent to India: I wanted to be in Europe when the war was won and Nazi Germany defeated. But once I was there, I found it fascinating and, to while away the boredom – we had no aircraft to train with – I started to write. (Later some of what I had written then was published under the title *Indian Route March*).

After a few months of idleness, in the excruciating heat of the spring, several of us were sent to the famous officers' training college in Poona. I completed my course successfully, except for one highly embarrassing incident which might easily have resulted in my dishonourable discharge from the college.

At 6 o'clock every morning we rehearsed the most complicated manoeuvres on the parade-ground in preparation for the march-past in front of a senior officer who 'took the salute' each week. I always found a place in the middle of the ranks so that I could just follow the others in their various movements while thinking about something more interesting. One fine Sunday morning the Regimental Sergeant-Major told me I was to have the honour of leading the parade. And it was to be a special honour, because a visiting American general who had been in 'Market Garden' was taking the salute and said he wanted to meet me. Before he had finished I blurted out, 'Oh no, Sir! I couldn't possibly. Please choose someone else.' The RSM simply ignored my pleading with a brisk 'There's no need to be modest, my good man. This is an order.'

The bugle sounded the fall-in, and the RSM shouted, 'Marker ... Out!' I marched out as smartly as I could and the rest followed. After that my mind went blank. Apparently I led the parade into a left wheel and then three right wheels, so that it cut off its own tail and was soon in complete disarray. The rest of the cadets were doubled up with hysterical laughter and couldn't even hold their rifles upright; they were mercifully released by the bugler desperately sounding the 'Retreat'.

I was summoned by the Commanding Officer. He addressed me in a quiet, resigned voice: 'What you did is so disgraceful that it has no precedent in the 200 years' history of this college. We have not yet been able to decide on a suitable punishment, but you may be sure that you will hear from me in due course. In the meantime, I never want to see you anywhere near the parade-ground again.'

Apparently no suitable-punishment was ever found, for I never heard any more about it. But from that time on I was excused every parade.

I passed my course, but at the end I did not wait for my official commission. Instead I went off to Calcutta. There, over a few beers in the Grand Hotel, I got into conversation with a naval officer who noticed the wings on my uniform and asked me about Arnhem.

He was Tony Clarkson, one of the editors of *Phoenix* magazine, published for the English-speaking troops of South-East Asia

Command. He showed me the current issue, which prominently featured extracts from a book published in England in January, *Arnhem Lift: Diary of a Glider Pilot*, by an anonymous writer. I quickly read some of the passages. It was my book! The title and publication date had been decided after I had left for India – this was the first I knew of it. Tony Clarkson was delighted; he had my photograph taken and published it in the next issue with a highly dramatised story about how they had found the anonymous author of *Arnhem Lift*.

A week later Tony Clarkson handed me a little red pass certifying that 'Lewis Haig', correspondent for *Phoenix*, should be given every assistance in obtaining information, transport, billets and finance. It was signed 'Louis Mountbatten, Commander-in-Chief, South-East Asia Command'.

After I had done features all over India on religious festivals, primitive jungle tribes, prostitution and British memsahibs, Tony told me that he was going to send me over to Burma, Malaya, Siam (now Thailand), Indonesia and Singapore. I was to write features and take photographs. When I said that I had only ever taken a few snaps with a Box Brownie years ago in Germany, he said it didn't matter. 'It will be much easier with the Leica you'll be taking with you. I'll be satisfied with one or two printable pictures in each reel of 36.'

So off I went, first to Rangoon, where I wrote a story about Major-General Orde Wingate,* the leader of the Chindits, a British irregular force that had operated behind Japanese lines in the mountainous Burmese jungle. Then I did a feature on Penang, the forces' dream holiday island, just off the Malayan mainland. From there I flew to Singapore and on to Bangkok on the heels of the retreating Japanese.

On my last assignment for *Phoenix* I was sent to Indo-China (now Vietnam). The French had occupied a large part of the country around the capital, Saigon, but in the north, Hanoi was held by a people's army, under their Moscow-trained leader, Ho Chi Minh.

---

* Wingate had been killed in an air crash in 1944.

They had fought the Japanese and were now fighting for their own independence from France. At this time there was an uneasy truce between Saigon, in the south, occupied by the Allies, and Hanoi in the north, ruled by Ho Chi Minh. I made friends with one of his senior advisers, a German communist, who arranged for me to interview Ho – the first western journalist to do so. Ho Chi Minh was surprisingly small and delicate; he answered every one of my questions courteously and to the point. To my astonishment he advocated co-operation with the western allies, saying, 'After all, we are both fighting the Japanese; though my people will never revert to their position under French colonial rule.'

I wrote a long feature advocating co-operation between the two regimes, but it was censored by the French authorities. France laid claim to the whole of Indo-China, a short-sighted policy that eventually resulted in the long and bloody Vietnam War.

After demobilisation I got a job on the Sunday Express in Berlin; later, Tony Clarkson, by then an editor with Odham's Press, sent me all over Germany to write for the weekly illustrated John Bull, and for Country Life. I used some of these articles for a book about the rise of Nazism called Follow my Leader (republished in paperback by Spellmount with the title Ein Volk, Ein Reich: Nine Lives Under the Nazis). This book tells the story of the Nazi regime – how it happened and why it happened – through interviews with ordinary Germans, instead of with their leaders. Later I wrote, edited and translated several other books, and in 1950 I started Primrose Film Productions with an office off Primrose Hill, near Regent's Park in London.

I now have two homes, one in England and one in Norway – my wife is a Norwegian painter – and we travel a lot, especially to Germany to visit what is left of my family. But England is my home, and if someone asks me what I am – German, Norwegian, Jewish or British – I answer, 'I'm an Englishman.'

EPILOGUE

The following is taken from Louis Hagen's unpublished autobiography.

I did not mean to attend the 50th anniversary of the battle. The idea of parading with hundreds of old veterans like myself, wearing rows of medals and red berets, did not appeal to me. But my publisher thought it was a good opportunity to promote the book. By the time he had persuaded me to attend, all the hotels and guest houses had been booked up and I was assigned to a billet in a barracks 30 miles outside Arnhem. Quite by chance, a retired nurse, Ans Kremer, helping in the town hall with the housing of thousands of veterans and their families, had read my book and recognised my name on the list. She immediately wrote to me, offering to put me up in her house in Oosterbeek, where most of the fighting had taken place. I was delighted to accept her invitation, particularly as she offered to fetch me from Amsterdam airport, 60km from Arnhem.

About 10 days before my departure, I was surprised to get a telephone call from someone who called himself Prince Bernhard of the Netherlands. I thought it was a practical joke, but he went on speaking in perfect German and using the familiar 'du' and I realised it really was Prince Bernhard. He complimented me on the book and said he wished I had spoken to him before I wrote the last chapter in which I blamed Field Marshal Montgomery for the disastrous failure of the airborne action. He said I had been too gentle. He and a Dutch major general had tried to warn Montgomery that the 9th and 10th Panzer Divisions were refitting near Arnhem. Montgomery had refused to listen. The presence of so many tanks had already been confirmed by listening to signals from the German High Command; Montgomery had also ignored these and had never passed on the information to the officers in charge of the Arnhem action. All this would indeed have been a valuable addition to the book. But what Prince Berhard was really telephoning for was to invite me to come to the palace when I arrived. Not thinking, I asked him for the address. He laughed: 'Oh, everybody knows where it is.' I explained that I was being met by Ans Kremer and her brother, and he told me to bring them, too. I did, and we all had tea in Prince Bernhard's study at the palace.

During the drive to Oosterbeek, Ans told me they were now almost certain they had met me 50 years ago when she had been 12 and her brother 10. They remembered the incredible moment when, after four years of German occupation, the sky above Oosterbeek was suddenly filled with hundreds of men and parachutes silently floating down. Mortars and shells started exploding all around and their parents had hustled them down into the cellar. On the third night there, they'd heard a persistent banging on the front door. Finally Ans's father thought he had better open it and Ans crept up after him. In the dark they saw a man in a uniform they did not recognise called out, 'Sprechen sie Deutsch?' then in perfect German asked if any of the houses were occupied by Germans: only then did they realise this was an Allied soldier come to liberate them. Now that she heard my voice, she thought I might have been that man. During the battle we had spent five days in the Kremer house; we used their heavy Victorian furniture to barricade the windows and dug trenches in the front and back gardens. When we got to their house, Stationsweg No 8, Ans fetched a battered, leather-bound visitors' book and opened it to a stained and blotchy page on which I had written, above the signature 'Lewis': 'I do hope and believe that the mess we made of your lovely house was worthwhile and good luck for a happier future.'

INDEX